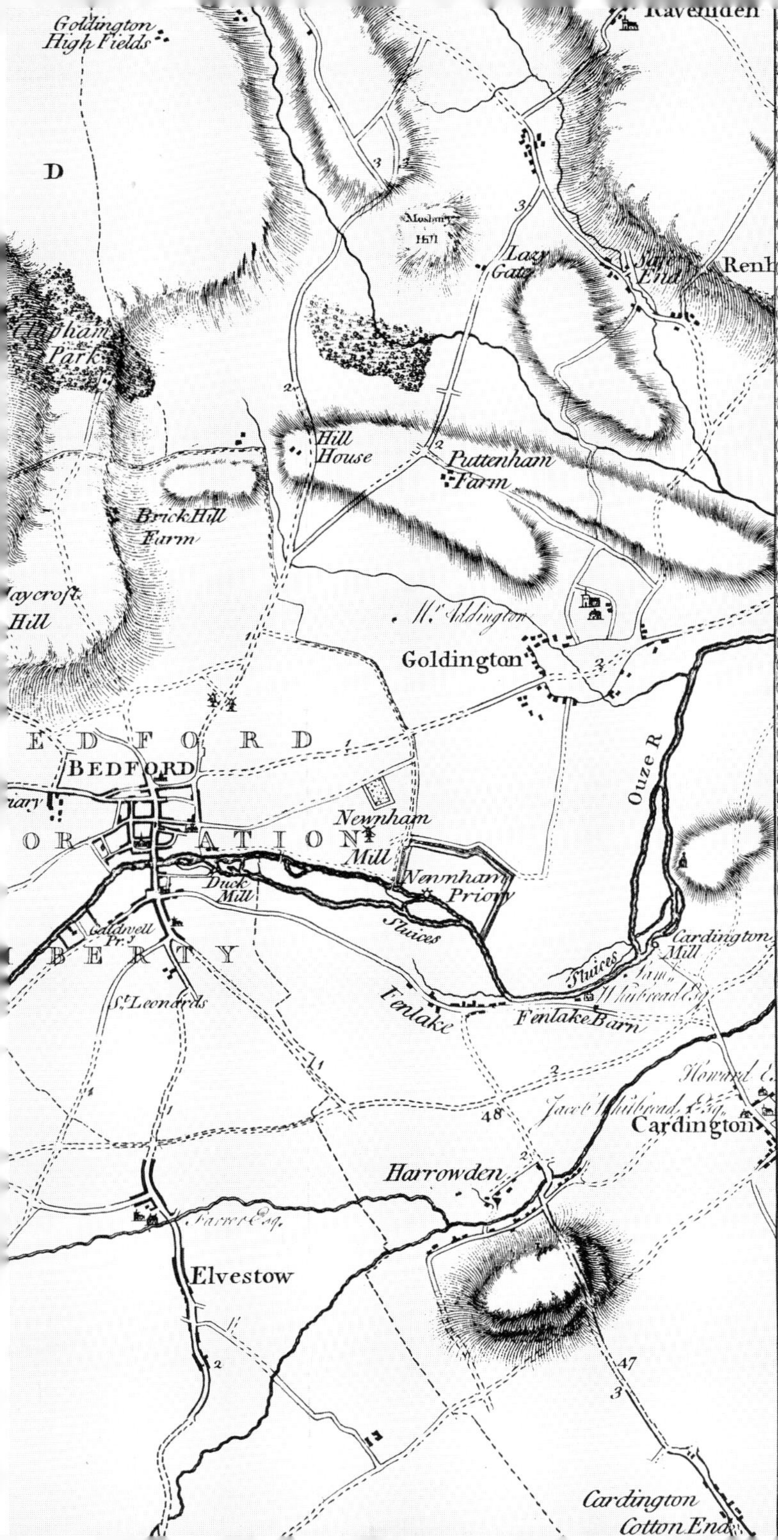

Goldington High Fields
Ravensden
D
Mosbury 1571
Lazy Gate
Salph End
Renh
Clapham Park
Hill House
Puttenham Farm
Brick Hill Farm
Haycroft Hill
Mr. Addington
Goldington
EDFORD
BEDFORD
ORPORATION
BERTY
Newnham Mill
Newnham Priory
Duck Mill
Caldwell Pr.y
Sluices
Ouze R.
Cardington Mill
St. Leonards
Fenlake
Fenlake Barn
Saml. Whitbread Esq.
Howard Esq.
Jacob Whitbread Esq.
Cardington
Harrowden
Farrer Esq.
Elvestow
Cardington Cotton End

Map of the Town of
BEDFORD
from Actual Survey in the Year
1841
To The Mayor Aldermen & Burgesses
of the
Borough of Bedford
THIS MAP
Is by permission most respectfully Dedicated
BY THEIR MUCH OBLIGED, AND MOST OBEDIENT SERVANT
M. Reynolds.
Scale of Feet
Scale of Chains
RUSSELL STREET
TAVISTOCK STREET
ALBERT STREET
PRINCE STREET
UNION STREET
OFFA STREET
CONDUIT STREET
FRIDAY TERRACE
ST. LOYES
DAME ALICE STREET
ST. PETER'S GREEN
LURKE LANE
HARPUR STREET
HIGH STREET
GREEN HILL STREET
THURLOE STREET
SILVER STREET
MILL STREET
DUKE STREET
CADEN STREET
THE GROVE
ST. PAUL'S SQUARE
St. Paul
Castle Hill
GOLDINGTON
POTTER STREET
CAULDWELL STREET
AMPTHILL STREET

BEDFORD PORTRAYED

GEORGE INN
POLHILL FOR EVER
THE PEOPLES CHOICE
WHITBREAD FOR EVER
CRAWLEY FOR EVER
WHITBREAD AND REFORM
POLHILL FOREVER
1835

BEDFORD PORTRAYED

Eighteenth and Nineteenth-Century Bedford Through Artists' Eyes

Preface by Halina Graham   Introduction by Richard Wildman   Commentary by Min Dinning

With photographs of present-day Bedford by Colin Kerr

CECIL HIGGINS ART GALLERY AND MUSEUM

1992

Dedicated to the citizens of Bedford, present and future, to inspire them to cherish their heritage

Castle Close
Bedford MK40 3NY

British Library Cataloguing in Publication Data
A catalogue record for this book is available from The British Library

ISBN 0 9512657 1 7

Photographs of historic Bedford are by Hawkley Studio Associates Ltd. All photographs of present-day Bedford are by Colin Kerr except nos 46 and 50 which are by Aerofilms Ltd and Tony Woodcock respectively.

All pictures are owned by the Borough of Bedford with the exception of the following: nos 1 and 12, Bedford County Record Office; no 51, Bedford Central Library ; no. 39, Luton Museum; no 4, Private Collection.

Design by Roger Davies
and set in Palatino on Ventura at The Green Street Press.
Printed by BAS, Over Wallop.

The captions for the photographs of present-day Bedford written by Colin Kerr.

References to present-day Bedford are correct at the time of printing, Summer 1992.

Page 1: Bradford Rudge, *The Bedford Times* (no. 54; see also page 82).

Page 2: Artist Unknown, *Bedford Town Elections* (no. 41; see also page 65).

Page 4: Artist Unknown, *The Swan Inn seen from the South Bank of the Ouse* (no. 7; see also page 21).

LIST OF PLATES

28 THOMAS FISHER
Saint Mary's Church, Bedford, from the S.W.
*c.*1820. Watercolour, 180 x 204 mm

29 THOMAS FISHER
Remains of S^t^. John's Hospital, Bedford
*c.*1820. Watercolour, 195 x 251 mm

30 THOMAS FISHER
S^t^. John's Church, Bedford
*c.*1820. Watercolour, 284 x 205 mm

31 THOMAS FISHER
Mr. Bunyans Meeting House Bedford & the Vestry in which his chair is preserved
*c.*1820. Watercolour, 202 x 247 mm

32 JOHN SUNMAN AUSTIN
Bunyans Meeting, Bedford, Beds.
1854. Tinted lithograph, 335 x 355 mm

33 JOHN SUNMAN AUSTIN
Howard Chapel, Bedford, Beds.
1854. Lithograph, 380 x 280 mm

34 THOMAS FISHER
Moravian Chapel, Bedford
c. 1820. Watercolour, 173 x 187 mm

35 BRADFORD RUDGE
Chapel & Ladies School &c. of the United Brethren, Bedford
*c.*1850. Lithograph, 297 x 389 mm

36 THOMAS FISHER
The Methodist Meeting in Angel Street, Bedford
*c.*1820. Watercolour, 184 x 220 mm

37 BRADFORD RUDGE
Wesleyan Methodist Chapel with Ministers House, and the Bedfordshire General Library
*c.*1840. Lithograph, 344 x 550 mm

38 THOMAS FISHER
High Street, Bedford
*c.*1820. Pencil sketch, entitled 'Street View, Bedford', 199 x 372 mm

39 THOMAS FISHER
Bedford County Jail
*c.*1820. Watercolour, from an interleaved copy of Lysons' *Bedfordshire* (1806), 220 x 318 mm

40 THOMAS FISHER
Sessions House & Town Hall, Bedford
*c.*1820. Watercolour, 201 x 242 mm

41 ARTIST UNKNOWN
Bedford Town Election
Dated 1835 but believed to depict the election of 1832. Oil on canvas, 618 x 755 mm

42 THOMAS FISHER
Bedford Infirmary
*c.*1820. Watercolour, 211 x 278 mm

43 JOHN SUNMAN AUSTIN
Infirmary and Fever Hospital, Bedford, Beds.
Dated 1850. Lithograph and watercolour, 492 x 670 mm

44 THOMAS FISHER
The Lunatic Asylum, Bedford
*c.*1820. Pencil sketch, 169 x 241 mm

45 FREDERICK GARNER
The Embankment
Dated 1886. Oil on canvas, 250 x 358 mm

46 HENRY BURN
Bedford from the North
*c.*1850-5. Coloured lithograph, 391 x 578 mm

47 LILIAN STANNARD
An Old Herbaceous Garden, Castle Close, Bedford
*c.*1901. Coloured lithograph cut from an unidentified magazine; based on an original watercolour, 240 x 352 mm

48 LT.-COL. GEORGE OLIVER RYBOT
18-26 Kimbolton Road
After 1872. Watercolour, 190 x 263 mm

49 LT.-COL. GEORGE OLIVER RYBOT
2-6 Goldington Road
After 1872. Watercolour, 191 x 266 mm

50 ARTIST UNKNOWN
Bedford Regatta, 1851
1851. Oil on canvas, 568 x 768 mm

51 ARTIST UNKNOWN
The Ouse Regatta
From *The Illustrated Times*, dated 31 August 1861. Wood engraving probably after a drawing by Edward Hull (1823-1905), 150 x 230 mm

52 ARTIST UNKNOWN
The Britannia Ironworks at Bedford
From an unidentified newspaper cutting, dated 14 July 1860. Coloured wood engraving, 86 x 356 mm

ARTIST UNKNOWN
Howard billhead
1839. Wood engraving, 189 x 231 mm

53 ARTIST UNKNOWN
Britannia Works from the North Side
Early 1860s. Coloured lithograph, 457 x 1230 mm

54 BRADFORD RUDGE
The Bedford Times
*c.*1846. Coloured lithograph, 402 x 550 mm.

PREFACE

HALINA GRAHAM

The purpose of this book is to bring to public attention the rich but little-known collection of views of Bedford, dating from the eighteenth and nineteenth centuries, in the possession of Bedford Borough Council. Its publication has been made possible first by the foresight of Bedford Borough Council, who allowed me access to the pictures stored in various places in the Town Hall. They subsequently agreed to the conservation of those most urgently in need of attention and, from 1978 onwards, to a programme of cleaning and conserving those which I considered would furnish the best illustrations to the proposed book. The Area Museums Service for South Eastern England helped to finance this programme; most of the oil-paintings and all the works on paper were conserved in their studios at Kenwood and the Fitzwilliam Museum, Cambridge, respectively. Their skills were particularly tested by *Bedford Town Election* (no.41) and *Bedford Regatta*, 1851 (no.50), which, it was discovered, had been cleaned at some time in the past by scrubbing with a substance which removed areas of the paint surface; the former was so difficult a case that it was shown to an international conference of oil conservators at the Courtauld Institute in London. A local historian has suggested a reason for their condition. Many years ago they hung in the Mayor's Parlour; he once knew a member of the Town Hall maintenance staff whose duties included cleaning the windows there, and he conjectured that having been ordered to clean first them and then the pictures the man had used the same materials for both tasks. A different problem was presented by John Sunman Austin's *Howard Chapel* (no.33), which was and is disintegrating because of the poor quality of the paper on which it was printed.

The publication of this book would not have been possible without the funds generously contributed by Mrs H. J. Casebourne, in memory of her cousin, Edward Taunton Williams (1874-1953). This is fitting, since Mr Williams was Clerk to Bedford Divisional Justices for thirty years, and to Sharnbrook Divisional Justices for fifteen. The Trustees of the Cecil Higgins Art Gallery, Humphrey Whitbread, Henry Bett and Hilary Guest, allowed me to use these funds for the publication of the book. I am delighted that the Governors of the Harpur Trust, which has played so large a part in the educational history of Bedford, financed the major part of the research.

Min Dinning carried out the research and wrote the text. Patricia Bell, formerly the County Archivist at the Bedfordshire County Record Office, and Richard Wildman were most generous in putting their knowledge of Bedford and its history at her disposal. Colin Kerr, an architect, took the photographs of present-day Bedford and wrote their captions. He often carried out the photography under considerable difficulties, sometimes standing on a ladder in the middle of a busy street or roundabout when a high wind was blowing in order to match his shots with the views of the original artists.

I would also like to acknowledge the assistance given by Professor Frank Lelièvre and Deborah Wakeling, who edited the text, Roger Davies, who designed the book, and contributed many ideas towards it; a private collector for allowing us to reproduce George Arnald's *The Demolition of Old Bedford Bridge* (no.4), the only illustration to come from a private collection; Anne Buck, Frank Branston, Ken Dickens, Simon Houfe, and John Wyatt; the staff of the County Record Office, Bedford, especially Sylvia Woods and Nigel Lutt; the staff at Bedford Museum, especially the Curator, John Turner; and all the staff at the Cecil Higgins Art Gallery, especially James B. Graham, Jennie

47 LILIAN STANNARD
An Old Herbaceous Garden, Castle Close, Bedford (detail).
See also page 72.

Clarke, Mickie Rausa, Gill Stafford and Caroline Bacon, who helped the project with great enthusiasm and dedication. Last, but by no means least, I would like to extend my warmest thanks to Sir David Wilson, former Director of the British Museum, for all the help and encouragement he has given me over the years with this and other projects.

The essential idea of this book occurred to me when I first came to Bedford in 1971. I was immediately attracted to the town and its associations with John Bunyan and John Howard. Many years later a journalist, Nigel Andrew, visited Bedford and recorded his impressions in an article in *The Times*, 'The Price of Progress' (5 August 1989), beginning with a well-chosen summary 'a place where beauty and ugliness compete for attention'. The town obviously made much the same impression on him as it did upon me, but he expressed it more elegantly than I could.

Bedford is a fascinating mixture of beauty and ugliness, almost a microcosm of the best and the worst possibilities of English urban life. Architecturally it has a bit of everything you would expect of a smallish historic town, but no spectacular highlights. The progress of post-war development can be followed with depressing clarity, the sore thumbs of the Sixties and Seventies giving way to the mildly-inflamed pinkies of the post-modern Eighties.
It is a familiar pattern, and it has seriously compromised the appearance of Bedford.

My curiosity about Bedford's townscape led me to wonder how the town had looked before the post-war development mentioned by Mr Andrew. I was sure that somewhere there must be pictures of Bedford as it used to be and over the years succeeded in locating them. To my surprise many were stored in Bedford Town Hall but not all were listed.

All the pictures illustrated except no.4 are in public collections in Bedfordshire.The Gallery possesses the preliminary sketches for two of the Thomas Fishers – *Bedford Castle – now a Bowling green* (no.1) and *Bedford County Jail* (no. 39) – but I preferred the finished watercolours owned by Bedfordshire County Record Office and Luton Museum respectively, as they are more informative. Since one of the purposes behind this book is to publicise lesser-known views of Bedford, some well-known examples, such as the watercolours of *Bedford Bridge* by J.M.W. Turner (Artemis Group) and Thomas Hearne (National Galleries of Scotland), have been deliberately omitted.

I have long considered that a permanent display of pictures and other material relating to Bedford's history would be very desirable, and I hope this book may be a step towards realizing this by appealing to those who want to know more about how and where their ancestors lived. I hope, too, it will create a renewed interest in views of historic Bedford and hence, perhaps, to the discovery of examples at present unknown. Finally, when Bedford's most historic area, that surrounding the Gallery, is developed, as it may soon be, this record of older times may help to ensure that as much as possible is left for future generations to enjoy.

INTRODUCTION

RICHARD WILDMAN

This is the first book principally devoted to a collection of old paintings, prints and drawings of Bedford to be published since 1951. In that year, as part of Bedford's contribution to the Festival of Britain, *A Picture Book of Bedford* was published from the Mayor's Parlour in the term of office of Richard Turner, Bedford's most antiquarian-minded mayor of modern times.

The text, and the captions to the illustrations, were by Christopher Carter (1884-1978), 'Touchstone' of the *Bedfordshire Times*. Artists represented included Bradford Rudge, John Sunman Austin, Henry Burn and Robert W. Fraser; some of the pictures were the same as in the present book, for most of the old views were in the collection of Bedford Corporation, housed in the Muniments Room under the eye of its keeper, Denis Gilmore, and various committee rooms of the Old Town Hall (the former Bedford Grammar School). The 1951 publication also included many old photographs, and ended with a 'Vision of the Future' by the architect and planner Max Lock, whose town-planning report *Bedford by the River* came out the following year.

The modern vision now appears inevitably rather out-of-date, whereas Carter's beautifully written essay can be seen as perhaps the last in a long tradition of antiquarian surveys of Bedford history, from the brothers Lysons (1806) and J.H. Matthiason (1831), through Blyth (1873), D.G. Cary Elwes (1881) and Carter's old mentor John Hamson (1896), to the occasional articles and lectures of his contemporaries Walter Henman and F.W. Kuhlicke. There was too much invention and whimsy in the books of the Rev. C.F. Farrar for their contents to be taken seriously as history, but *Old Bedford* (1926) included a fine collection of old views of the town. In more recent years the authoritative histories of Bedfordshire, the Harpur Trust and Bedford itself by Joyce Godber, firmly based on archival sources, have been published in well-illustrated editions.

Now Min Dinning has described a variety of Bedford pictures, most of which come from the collection of Bedford Borough Council, successor to Bedford Corporation. On the initiative of the Curator, Halina Graham, these have been deposited in the Cecil Higgins Art Gallery and Museum for reasons of safe-keeping, conservation and research.

Some are considerable works of art in their own right, such as William Henry Pyne's *The Pig Market in the yard of the Fountain Inn* (no.13), which has long been a favourite among exhibits in the Gallery, and George Arnald's *The Demolition of Old Bedford Bridge* (no.4). There are others which are works of high quality by local artists, like Thomas Jobson Jackson's two views of the riverside (nos 9 and 10) and Robert W. Fraser's *Old Duck Mill* (no.11). The two paintings of the old Swan Inn (nos 6 and 7), the one of its replacement, the present Swan Hotel (no.8) and that of the 1835 election (no.41) – all by unknown artists – are important historical documents as well as being charming by virtue of their naïvety. Thomas Fisher's watercolours of Bedford churches and public buildings and his marvellous sketch of the High Street (no.38) recall late Georgian Bedford, whilst the prints of Bradford Rudge and John Sunman Austin evoke the mid-nineteenth-century town. Rudge has always been appreciated, so it is good to see Sunman Austin well represented too. In my view he is at least Rudge's equal as a topographical artist, but his unhappy life and abrupt departure from Bedford, together with his death in Oxford, had obscured his importance.

These artists and most of the others included in this book must have had some inner compulsion to record the Bedford they saw. Thomas Fisher is one obvious example. A few of them worked on

46 HENRY BURN
Bedford from the North.
See also page 71.

commission from publishers, but in almost every case a love of the subject-matter is evident.

It is more than twenty years since the last exhibition of items from the Corporation's collection was held in the Bedford Gallery adjoining the Cecil Higgins in Castle Lane (in 1970). At about that time Castle Lane was being cleared of its remaining buildings in preparation for a multi-storey car-park which did not materialise. At the time of writing the Castle Lane area is on the brink of being built up again with shops, offices, flats, a multi-storey car-park, library and theatre. The improver's hand may reach out to the Castle Mound itself.

This venerable relic, painted by Fisher, is the first picture in Min Dinning's book. For longer than any other surviving Bedford structure (except perhaps the tower of St Peter's Church) it has been a witness to the changes to which Bedford has been subjected in over 900 years, some of the most drastic occurring only in the last forty. The pleasing decay which, as shown in this book, attracts and inspires artists does not usually appeal to civic authorities and the world of commerce. Yet it was a highly astute businessman – Cecil Higgins – who founded the Gallery, housed after his death, by a happy chance, in his old family home. The late Victorian enclave of Castle Close is a remarkable and precious survival, with much of the character observed by Lilian Stannard (no.47) still intact. Despite impending changes to the immediate vicinity, I hope it will so remain into the next century.

THE PLATES

45 FREDERICK GARNER *The Embankment*. See also page 70.

1 THOMAS FISHER

Bedford Castle – now a Bowling green

*c.*1820. Watercolour, 220 x 270 mm

This quiet abandoned spot was the site of one of the most turbulent episodes in Bedford's history — the siege of Bedford Castle in 1224.

Following the Norman Conquest a castle was built in Bedford by Ralf de Tallebosc. Probably consisting of a wooden tower on an artificial mound, it was built straddling the eastern boundary of the town on the north bank of the River Ouse. De Tallebosc's daughter married into the Beauchamp family who then held the castle for over a century. While the castle flourished, it dominated the town and was later rebuilt in stone. During the troubled reign of King Stephen, however, conflicts broke out between the Beauchamps and the King, and the castle was seized. The family later returned, and in 1153 the castle was used as a refuge by King Stephen's men against Prince Henry (later Henry II).

When the barons gathered in Bedford and plotted against King John in 1215, he sent a ruthless mercenary, Falkes de Breauté, to attack the castle. Falkes took it, and installed huge fortifications, including stone-lined ditches, demolishing the local churches of St Paul's and St Cuthbert's to use their stone for his works. Meanwhile he gained a local reputation for all kinds of villainy. Henry III eventually sent his forces, and the famous siege of Bedford Castle took place in June-July 1224. For six weeks Falkes's men held out against the King's, but finally the defeated inhabitants of the castle surrendered. Eighty men were hanged, and Falkes, who had not been present at the siege, was banished. The fortifications of the castle were destroyed to prevent any future incidents, and eventually the site was reduced to rubble.

The site belonged to the Mowbrays in the fourteenth century and was described as a 'void plot' in 1361. By 1399 it was worth ten shillings and was 'neither built on nor inclosed'. This apparently worthless site changed hands several times after that. In the sixteenth century some remnants of the castle still existed, when John Leland reported 'a great round hill which was a burrow for foxes', and William Camden reported 'ruins overhanging the river'.

Some time in the sixteenth century a bowling-green was made on top of the flattened mound, which continued in use for more than three centuries and was still called 'The Bowling Green' in a plan of 1908. For centuries bowling was a popular sport enjoyed by all levels of society. In about 1702 Celia Fiennes, the diarist, visited Bedford and wrote:

> ... [the river] runns by a ground which is made into a fine bowling-green, its upon a hill and a pretty ascent from the river that is besett with willows all round beneath; the bowling-green is well kept with seates and summer houses in it for the use of the Town and Country Gentlemen of which many resort to it especially the Market dayes ...

Fisher's picture shows the spot from the south-east as it looked in the early nineteenth century. The path leading to a gate on the left must have led towards Castle Lane. The small hut on the south side of the mound was later replaced by an Edwardian summer-house, which was demolished in about 1968.

The Higgins family, who bought the site of the castle in 1908, had already built a brewery and a house to the north of the mound, and cut an ice-house into its north side. The house and grounds were offered to the Corporation in 1909 at a price much below the market value, but it was not until 1924 that Bedford Corporation bought it for £4,350. Today the mound's slopes are covered with trees.

Castle Mound from the south-west across the Ouse. The proposed office development (1992) would completely obscure this view of the mound.

2 GEORGE NOBLE

Bedford Bridge

1790s. Woodblock print, 188 x 230 mm

There was probably a ford across the Ouse in this area from the earliest times. The date of the first bridge is not known, but it would have been made of wood. When the old stone bridge was taken down in 1811 before the rebuilding:

> Workmen engaged on the foundations of the present bridge [completed 1813] found Roman coins and rose nobles of Edward III besides antiquities ... Some pieces of oak were also found in a good state of preservation, capable of taking a fine polish, from which fine boxes were made as curios.
>
> R.B. Hankin: *An Account of the Public Charities of the Town of Bedford* (1828)

The first stone bridge was known as 'The Great Bridge'. Several rather similar pictures exist, the best known being Noble's engraving, which is undated. Since it shows two buildings on the bridge, it depicts the structure as it looked before 1765, the year in which both buildings were demolished in order to ease the passage of traffic. Noble's picture shows the bridge from the east, from a point on or near the north bank of the river. It was 100 metres long and 4 metres wide, with a parapet 1 metre high. In the centre are two buildings: a toll gate to the south (left), which was also used for storing arms and gunpowder for the county militia; and to the north another larger building, thought to have been on the site of the Chantry Chapel of St Thomas, built about 1331, beneath which, and projecting to the east side, was the room used for a time as the Town Gaol. This is one of Bedford's most famous sites, though long demolished. It used to be thought that this was where John Bunyan (see no. 31) was imprisoned and dreamed his famous dream in 1676, which inspired him to write *The Pilgrim's Progress*. This belief (no longer held by historians) is commemorated by a plaque on the present bridge. The exact location of St Thomas's Chapel is uncertain as old references to it sometimes suggest that it was close to the bridge rather than on it.

By the 1760s the original construction had been repaired several times and partially rebuilt as the river was subject to regular flooding resulting in frequent damage. At the north end of the bridge, on the right, the old Swan Inn can be seen behind a wall. Two men in a rowing-boat, carrying sacks upstream, may be dealing in corn or coal, as Bedford was the head of the navigable part of the Ouse by the eighteenth century. Other versions show differently dressed men with cargoes of barrels, possibly containing salt fish or sugar.

3 WILLIAM HENRY PYNE

Bedford Bridge from the South East

*c.*1807. Watercolour, 371 x 498 mm

This is a favourite view of Bedford and has been drawn by many different artists, including Walker and Thomas Hearne, but Pyne's picture is probably the most famous. It appears on Brayley's map of 1807 as a vignette. The watercolour may have been made in preparation for the subsequent engraving. Pyne would have stood on Green's Wharf, beside what is now the Mallards Bar and Brasserie, near the river bank.

The central feature, St Paul's Church, standing somewhat higher above the bridge in Pyne's view than it does above the modern bridge today, can, of course, still be seen, though the tower and spire were rebuilt in 1868. The bridge itself has changed: the one depicted is the old bridge which was demolished in 1811, shortly after the picture was painted. The narrow arches and heavy buttresses allowed the river to silt up, and reeds grew in mid-river impeding the passage of boats. John Wing's new higher Town Bridge replaced it in 1811-13 (see no. 4).

Pyne gives us an interesting view of the old buildings on the space opposite the Swan Inn. These extended from the bridge to the corner of St Paul's Square, then known as Vine's Corner. They were later replaced by Bank Buildings, named after Barnard's Bank, which was an office-block with shops built in 1855. When the Town Bridge was widened in 1938, Bank Buildings was pulled down and not replaced. The area is still known as the Bank Buildings site.

To the extreme right the George Inn is visible on the site now occupied by Swan Court office-block (1959-60) which today includes the Guardian Royal Exchange Insurance office and Deep Pan Pizza restaurant. Before the arrival of the railway water traffic was the only way to transport heavy loads. Boats brought sea-borne coal and timber to King's Lynn, and from there barges brought them up the Ouse. By 1689 barges were able to reach Bedford, and merchants dealt in the products arriving from King's Lynn, sending grain downriver.

The new bridge by John Wing, completed 1813.

4 GEORGE ARNALD A.R.A.

The Demolition of Old Bedford Bridge, built 1224

Dated 1812. Oil on canvas, 700 x 1230 mm

This interesting and historic picture was originally sold by the artist to Samuel Whitbread in 1812 at a suggested price of '60 gns. or what S. W. likes'. The high price shows that Arnald had a considerable reputation at the time. The picture was exhibited at the Royal Academy in 1812.

Although the scene is recognisably Bedford, with St Paul's tower and spire and the three-gabled building on the Bank Buildings site identifiable, the 'Greek Temple' in the background is a fiction. Arnald seems to have created this large imposing building to give interest to the composition. It would have been near to the site of the old Georgian Sessions House (1753), on the south side of St Paul's Square, and may have been an idealised version of it. This device lends a fashionable neo-classical air to the scene and elevates the tone of what might otherwise seem to be a more 'technical' subject. The combination of neo-classicism and construction work is an interesting one, since it brings together two important facets of early nineteenth-century thinking: the admiration of the perfection of ancient style, and the practicality of rebuilding and developing our provincial towns in the early years of industrial expansion.

The Bedford Improvement Act of 1803 was an ambitious attempt to legislate for a rebuilding programme in the centre of town. The bridge was a subject of some controversy: while some people argued that 'because Parts of the Bridge are got to Pieces with great difficulty, that the whole structure was sound, and that there was no necessity for a new Bridge', the Commissioners asked John Wing, the architect and builder, to report on its condition. Naturally, as the person to whom the contract was likely to be awarded, Wing pronounced the bridge 'in a dilapidated and ruinous state'. He points out the bridge's defects in a letter of November 1809 and advises against merely widening the old structure, as he would not be able to guarantee its safety. This view is endorsed in 1811 by a London surveyor, George Cloake, who describes the weak structure of the old bridge:

> Very little hard stone has been used ... There appears to have been a sort of Rib formed in the Arches of Welldon Stone, and the Rubble filled in between, and a great body of Rubbish filled in over the Arches, so that time has made it a sort of Solid Mass.

The main material used for the rebuilding was stone from Branley Fell in Yorkshire. This was well before the days of the railway, and materials would probably have been brought to the site by barge up the river.

The new bridge cost £15,137. It was so expensive that loans were needed to complete the work. Samuel Whitbread and the 6th Duke of Bedford each lent £2,000, and the Marquis of Bute lent £1,000. Twenty-four other 'county gentry' made smaller contributions. The bridge was completed amid much controversy by 1813, and tolls had to be charged to help recoup the cost, though the Whitbreads and some others made their loans into gifts.

In the picture not much demolition work seems to be going on. Thomas Blyth mentions 'an excellent temporary wooden [bridge] which cost £400 being constructed ad interim', but there is no sign of this. It went from Green's Wharf to the area in front of the Swan, and possibly the artist stood upon it to make his sketch for this picture.

5 J. H. MATTHIASON

Bedford Bridge with Swan Inn and Gardens

Dated 1824. Coloured lithograph by Robert Havell, jun., 382 x 538 mm

J.H. Matthiason, who taught mathematics at the English, or Commercial, School (now Bedford Modern School), was the author and illustrator of *Bedford and Its Environs* (1831), a sympathetic account of the town where he met many difficulties. This book, which contains small, almost primitive illustrations of local views, is a thorough, painstaking description of Bedford, its buildings and institutions, but the author's comments demonstrate his radical, open outlook, and he eloquently defends education for all, particularly for women. He pleads also for a relaxation in the game laws, and describes with disgust a public execution. The black and white pictures illustrating the book, though stylish, are rather quaint compared with the refinement of this picture of Bedford Bridge on the River Ouse with the Swan Inn and gardens. It is possible, though, that the delicacy of this view may owe something to the lithographer, Robert Havell, jun.

Made in 1824, this charming lithograph is dedicated as follows: 'To Francis Green Esq., Mayor and the other Members of the Corporation of Bedford, this view on the Ouse is most respectfully inscribed by their obliged and devoted humble servant J. H. Matthiason', possibly in the hope of a helpful patron.

This view would have been from a boat on the river. The 'handsome modern bridge' described in the artist's book is the central feature. The Swan Inn to the right was still a showpiece in Bedford, being one of the town's largest buildings at the time, and the gardens were a delightful spot in which elegant people could relax. Above the drinking horse is a small building, just visible through the Swan's side gateway. This was the toll-house for the new bridge, opened in 1813, and it eventually became Bedford's first Post Office when the toll was removed in 1835.

Beyond the toll-house are some sheds belonging to the wharves on the river. To the left (the south bank) are more wharves and maltings. This side of the bridge, on the site of the Moat House Hotel, was Green's Wharf where coal, wood and iron were brought from King's Lynn, while the site of Nash's Maltings, which used to be on the west side, was later occupied by the Bridge Hotel, demolished in 1980. Green's Wharf belonged to the family of the Mayor to whom the picture is dedicated.

6 ARTIST UNKNOWN

View of the Swan Inn, looking South across Bedford Bridge

*c.*1790. Oil on canvas, 420 x 525 mm

This delightful oil-painting is one of three pictures depicting the Swan Inn in the late eighteenth century. The style suggests that the artist may have been a sign-painter, but his identity is not known.

The old Swan Inn was much closer to the bridge than the present building, and the bridge depicted is the old one which was demolished in 1811. The Inn itself was an established Bedford landmark, appearing on old maps, and is mentioned in a document of 1507 as 'a tenement called Swan'. It has been claimed that the earliest building on the site was built partly with stones from the ruins of Bedford Castle. These 'ruines' are shown on Speed's map of 1610, near to the site of the Swan, where the castle used to be.

There are many Swan Inns in Bedfordshire and Buckinghamshire, which were both in the diocese of Lincoln, and St Hugh of Lincoln was often depicted with a tame swan.

The picture shows a two-storey building with smoking chimneys, a central entrance to the inn yard, and an upstairs bay window overlooking the north end of the bridge, beneath which are steps down to the water. There may have been gates at the entrance once, but 'an Horrible and unheard-of tempest' flung off the gates in 1672, and it is not clear whether they were replaced. A wrought-iron sign with a painting of a swan stands outside the bay window. The narrow bridge arches over the river, and on the south bank St Mary's Church is visible, which it is not today, as the intervening tall buildings obscure it.

A busy scene is portrayed. A chaise with a single horse stands outside the inn. This type of small coach, which was a popular mode of transport until the 1820s, is likely to have been a private chaise as it held only one passenger. Though this predates the famous Bedford Times coach (see no. 54), a public passenger coach operated thrice weekly from 1785, and mail was regularly carried to and from London.

Today the site is dominated by the high-rise Moat House Hotel on the south bank, and the present Swan Hotel at the north end of the bridge. With a constant flow of traffic, the association of this spot with travel and hospitality is still very obvious.

The weathervane of St Mary's Church is just visible to the left of the street light on the bridge.

7 ARTIST UNKNOWN

The Swan Inn seen from the South Bank of the Ouse

c.1790. Oil on canvas, 422 x 523 mm

This view of the Swan Inn from the south bank shows the full extent of quite a large building. The style suggests that it may have been painted by the same artist and at about the same date as no. 6. It was here in 1661 that Elizabeth, John Bunyan's second wife, pleaded for her husband's release from prison, where he had been sent for preaching without a licence.

The inn's close proximity to the river would have meant plenty of good fresh fish. Celia Fiennes, the diarist, visited Bedford early in the eighteenth century. She says that the Ouse is:

... stored with very good fish, and those which have gardens on its brinke keepes a sort of trunck or what they call them (its a receptacle of wood of a pretty size full of holes to let the water in and out) here they keep fish they catch as pike perch tench etc., so they have it readye for their use; this is of mighty advantage especially for the Publicke houses, you see the fish taken out fresh for supper or dinner ... these truncks or baskets which keepes the fish are fastned by chaines to the sides of the banks ...

In 1806 the brothers Lysons reported many varieties of fish in the river and remarked on the 'bleak' (small river fish) around the town bridge.

On the left the bay window is visible with the sign of the Swan outside, and the steps to the river's edge beneath.

The cargo barge (bottom right) was either a sailing-vessel or horse-towed. Stoves were used to warm the crew accommodation, and smoke is coming out of the chimney. At that time the river was the usual thoroughfare for transporting goods. By 1689 lighters could reach Bedford by river from King's Lynn through a system of locks with tolls. Cargoes in the eighteenth century would have been coal from Newcastle by way of King's Lynn, timber from Scandinavia and other building materials, grain, salt, fish, iron and a variety of other useful products. After 1689 Bedford had coal wharves from which coal was distributed to surrounding areas. Lighters returning to the coast would often carry agricultural produce, still an important product of the area.

To the right of the inn the Castle Mound is just visible, and on it was Bedford's famous bowling-green behind the inn. The old inn must have been damp and chilly and eventually have become dilapidated. The 5th Duke of Bedford bought the old Swan in 1787. Shortly after this picture was painted it was demolished, and a splendid new inn was built in its place (see no. 8).

8 ARTIST UNKNOWN

The Swan Inn from the South West as rebuilt in 1794

*c.*1796. Oil on canvas, 413 x 597 mm

This painting of the Swan Inn, which shows the building which replaced the inn in nos 6 and 7, is seen from the south-west, near the south end of the Town Bridge.

In 1794 Francis, 5th Duke of Bedford, commissioned the building of the new Swan Inn. Henry Holland (1745-1806), a famous architect who worked for the Duke at Woburn Abbey from 1787 to 1792, designed the Georgian building with Ionic columns supporting an imposing portico. The stonework was carried out by John Wing at a cost of £1,022.13s.11d. Originally from Leicestershire, Wing had also been employed on the Duke's estate at Woburn. The Duke decided to dismantle Houghton House at Ampthill, thought to be the inspiration for Bunyan's 'House Beautiful', and use parts of it for the construction of the Swan. Wing brought 'chimnie pieces' from Houghton, and, among other useful materials, a splendid staircase which can still be seen. It is claimed to be the one which inspired a staircase ascending to Bunyan's 'Chamber of Peace', as he may have seen it at Houghton House.

John Wing (1756-1826) undertook many building projects in Bedford at the end of the eighteenth and during the first quarter of the nineteenth centuries. A prominent member of the community, he was Mayor in 1793, 1808 and 1817, and a very successful local architect and builder.

As mentioned by Celia Fiennes and the brothers Lysons, Bedford was known then for good fishing (see no. 7). The silted islets with reeds growing on them were cleared when Wing built the new Town Bridge in 1811-13 (see no. 4).

The George Inn is just visible on the left. The two inns had opposing political allegiances, the George being the Tory house and the Swan the Whig stronghold (see no. 41).

9 THOMAS JOBSON JACKSON

Early morning on the Bedford Ouse

1889. Oil on canvas, 447 x 647 mm

Jackson's delight in his adopted town is evident in his pictures. This idyllic, lush view of the Ouse, looking towards St Paul's Church from a rural pathway on the south bank, suggests a fresh, leafy, damp morning in early summer. An abundance of trees on the north bank above the site of the old Barnard's Coal Wharf, with the church tower and spire emerging in splendour, is a very different scene from the one visible today. Seen from an asphalt path near Mander College, the view across the river now displays far fewer trees and many more buildings. The trees on the left were felled for the building of Charles Wells's Brewery, which was demolished in 1976, and those in the centre were in the garden of the Head Master of Bedford Grammar

School, which is now the site of the Town Hall office-block. The Horne Lane market-place and the Town Hall now dominate the scene, and although some buildings are matched in proportion with the Shire Hall of 1881, others are unmistakably mid-twentieth century and obscure the tower and spire of St Paul's Church to a point where the view is almost unrecognisable.

Painted in 1889, the picture owes something to Jackson's artistic imagination, since one would have expected to see the edge of the 1881 Shire Hall on the far right. He may well have decided that it would spoil the timeless calm of his composition. A punt in the foreground, moored by a rural path with wild flowers growing near it, suggests the leisurely aspect of the river, which is fortunately still one of the features of the Ouse at Bedford, although this part of the river bank no longer has grassy paths.

10 THOMAS JOBSON JACKSON

Mill Meadow

1879. Oil on canvas, 344 x 516 mm

The weeping willow by the river bank and the green meadows make this picture of Mill Meadows look familiar. Painted before the Russell Park end of The Embankment was formally established as an area for public recreation, the scene seems rural and far from the bustle of the busy town that Bedford had become by 1879. It is, however, only a five-minute walk from the centre of town and from the two schools where the young fishermen may have been pupils. Grammar School boys were allowed to fish in the river, and the area around Mill Meadows, beyond Duck Mill, from which the name derives, would have been near enough for an excursion after school.

The boys in their straw hats remind one of the young William Hale White ('Mark Rutherford') who spent idyllic summer days by the river in Bedford:

> ... on summer Wednesdays and Saturdays we wandered along its banks for miles, alternately fishing and bathing. I remember whole afternoons in June, July and August, passed half-naked or altogether naked in solitary meadows and in the water; ... I remember, too, the place where we used to swim across the river with our clothes on our heads, because there was no bridge near, and the frequent disaster of the slip of the braces in the middle of the water, so that shirt, jacket, and trousers were soaked, and we had to lie on the grass in the broiling sun without a rag on us till everything was dry again.

The river seems narrower and less controlled than it is today. The banks are supported, and there are asphalt paths where Jackson's schoolboys would have strolled on grassy, muddy tracks. Weeds and grasses thrive at the water's edge, where now there are neat stones to support the river bank.

The distance reveals no building to interrupt the impression of a country scene. Jackson might have felt a certain nostalgia in such a view. An active, sporting countryman at heart, he would have found fishing a relaxing summer pastime. Today, too, many people fish on the banks of the Ouse, and the area is still a favourite spot for outings. The Embankment upstream from the Suspension Bridge is planted with formal gardens on the north side. Russell Park has paths and a sports pavilion, and football is played there at weekends. Boating clubs and school rowing teams use the river regularly, and it is fortunate that this part of town retains its peaceful charm.

Near Russell Park with Mill Meadows on the opposite bank.

Duck Mill. The sluices above which the mill was built can be clearly seen in this photograph.

11 ROBERT W. FRASER

Old Duck Mill

1885. Watercolour, 370 x 578 mm

This view painted by Fraser looks south-west, from a boat on the river. Fraser and his brothers often painted the River Ouse and knew it well. This painting shows his awareness of the details of the spot and affection for a very familiar place.

The old Duck Mill, which had been in existence since at least the eleventh century, was demolished some time after the picture was painted. The corn mill made use of the swift-flowing waters of the Ouse, and was located above the sluices which can still be seen near Duck Mill Bridge. The site has no buildings on it now but is part of a pathway for walking along the south bank of the river.

For many centuries the mill ground the corn into flour for bread for the townspeople of Bedford. Many watermills existed along the Ouse until relatively recent times. On the north bank to the east of the bridge stood the Port Mills, and Newnham Mill was in Goldington. In 1506 there was a mill driven by horsepower in St Cuthbert's, which is why 'Schole Lane' (so named because the Grammar School was there before the Reformation) eventually became Mill Lane, then Mill Street. By the late nineteenth century Duck Mill had turned to steam-power, but the property was bought by Bedford Corporation, which was extending pleasure-grounds on both sides of the

river. The ancient buildings were pulled down before 1891, though the sluices are still there. The only other reminder of the Mill's existence is the name given to the footbridge, a nearby block of flats and Duck Mill Lane, which leads down to the area from south of the Town Bridge. This name, introduced in the 1860s, replaces an older one, 'Buoy and Oar Lane', named after a nearby public house, demolished when Wing rebuilt the bridge.

While the miller Benjamin Harrison was still in charge of the mill, and the ancient tradition of corn-grinding continued, there must have been a timeless quality about this area which separated it from the busy Victorian residential town that Bedford had become. Its demolition helped change Bedford for ever. Fraser's charming picture is perhaps the best-known representation of this popular subject for local artists.

Old George Yard from the other (west) side. Some medieval rubble walling survives from the Old George Inn. Old stone was reused to form window reveals and quoins in the 1937 rebuilding. The site is a Scheduled Ancient Monument.

12 JOHN CARTER

George Inn Yard

Inscribed *'East View of an antient Edifice in the George Inn yard at Bedford (appears to have been an Entrance or Gateway) but sayd to have been a chapel dedicated to St. George'.*

Dated 1783. Pen and ink, 303 x 365 mm

Carter's drawing shows the inside of the George Inn Yard. Old photographs of the site confirm that Carter's 'East View' is from the High Street side looking westwards, into the main courtyard of the inn, with a small yard between the street and the archway. There were two George Inns in Bedford High Street — one next door to the Swan Inn by the north end of the bridge, and this one, often called the Old George, where part of Debenhams store is now located. This picture is typical of Carter's style, indicating his liking for Gothic architecture and a humorous group of figures.

The scene suggests a rural location, though in the centre of town. The 'antient Edifice' referred to by the artist is the building which has a small statue in a niche above a gateway. Carter explains that this 'appears to have been an Entrance or Gateway but sayd to have been a Chapel dedicated to St. George', and reminds us of the historical associations of the site. The inn was in existence by the fifteenth century and belonged to the Prior of Newnham. In 1806 the brothers Lysons described it thus: 'The Gothic building in the George-Yard is nothing more than part of the original structure of that ancient inn, which is spoken of by the same name in a record of the year 1481.' The statue in the niche portrayed St George, after whom the inn was named. The statue still existed in the early years of this century but had become almost entirely weathered away.

At some time during the eighteenth century the inn yard was used for the performance of plays such as *The Busy Body*, *The Wonder* and *The Jealous Wife*, so it must have been lively, but perhaps not the most elegant place in town. In 1792, however, it was used by the congregation of Mill Street Baptist Church. The inn closed in 1928, and the 'antient Edifice', which had not been occupied for generations, was demolished after 1937. Fragments of the ground floor, including the inner north side of the archway shown in the picture, may still be seen behind Debenhams. It is sad that this historic building was allowed to become dilapidated and the statue lost, and that it is now replaced by the outbuildings of a modern store.

St Mary's Church.

13 WILLIAM HENRY PYNE

The Pig market in the yard of the Fountain Inn, Bedford, with St. Mary's Church in the background

Dated 1806. Watercolour, pencil and some bodycolour, 328 x 482 mm

The Bedford pig market was held south of the river at St Mary's from the sixteenth century, and this lively picture celebrates the occasion. Pyne skilfully combines an elegant background with St Mary's Church and a busy scene in the inn yard.

Although it is early in the day, many people have made the journey from the villages to buy and sell, and some are still arriving through the entrance in Potter Street, which is now Cardington Road. Some are already drinking ale at 1½d. a pint, at the Fountain Inn. The Inn existed as early as 1606 under the name of the Red Lion, later becoming the Fountain, and the yard behind was the site of the Tuesday pig market until 1813.

The land is today occupied by the former Sun Life Assurance building on the corner of St Mary's Street and Cardington Road. The cream-painted building on the left with a red-tiled roof can be seen in a photograph of the 1870s, but this old inn was demolished in the 1890s, and its replacement was pulled down in 1967, when the Sun Life building was erected where the yard used to be. It is thus now impossible to see St Mary's Church from the exact spot where Pyne stood. He has altered the proportions of the church to make the tower seem taller and narrower, but in other respects it is not much changed, except for the lower tower window, which has since been opened up. A south aisle was added to the left of the tower in 1853. Since 1990 St Mary's Church has been Bedfordshire County Council's Archaeology Centre.

Men, women and children are all present for the market. Some countrywomen wear red cloaks, a mark of prosperity in Bedfordshire in those days. The market seems fairly informal, with everyone choosing his own place. Pigs were widely reared in the early nineteenth century. Berkshires, Tamworths and crosses between Suffolks and spotted Leicesters were the usual breeds, and a family would often keep a pig in their cottage garden, killing it themselves to make sausages, black puddings and hams. For those who did not keep their own pig fresh pork could be bought at 8d. a pound, and salt pork was a shilling, which was fairly expensive in 1806.

W. H. Pyne 1806

14 THOMAS FISHER

St. Paul's Church and New Market Place

*c.*1820. Watercolour, 221 x 280 mm

This view from the south end of the High Street and the north-east corner of St Paul's Square can still be identified more than 170 years after the picture was painted. Although the tower and spire of the church were reconstructed in 1868, the shape remains the same as it was in Fisher's day. Another building, now occupied by Ladbroke's, the betting shop, stands where the one on the right of the picture stood, but it is of the same proportions as the old one. Fisher's rather stiff figures are unusual in that he rarely included people in his pictures, preferring to concentrate on the buildings.

Before the beginning of work resulting from the Bedford Improvement Act of 1803, St Paul's Square was a maze of houses and shops. It was dirty and badly paved, and the surrounding alleys were congested and insanitary. It had been the site of the butchers' and fishmongers' markets for many centuries, the different products being sold in their own special areas, with 'Fishrowe' to the east of the churchyard and 'Butchersrowe' to the north-east. The latter was demolished under the Act, and the new Butchers' Shambles, designed by John Wing and erected in 1804-5 can be seen here. The two red-brick buildings with slate roofs and a central wrought-iron gateway are two of the three sections of the new Shambles, as described in 1831 by J.H. Matthiason:

> ... a plain and commodious erection, more indeed for use than show, containing three sections of shops, or covered stalls; two running parallel with each other on each side of the gate, being joined at the end at right angles by the third which is the butter and poultry market; being well adapted by its cool and airy condition for the purpose intended ...

Speed's map shows that in 1610 the poultry market was on the south side of the square and the 'Moute Hall', or Guildhall, was on the east. The site of the old Guildhall was in front of the wrought-iron gates, but the Improvement Commissioners demolished it in 1806, intending to rebuild it. Their funds ran out, however, all available funds for town improvements being channelled to the expensive rebuilding of the Town Bridge.

Matthiason's description continues:

> In front of the market house, on a quadrangular area called the market hill, is the fruit and vegetable market, which however, particularly in busy seasons, generally extends by the side of the footway for half the distance through the town.

St Paul's Church and former Market Square.

The Shambles was demolished in 1849 to allow the erection of a Corn Exchange, renamed the Floral Hall when the present Corn Exchange was built. The Floral Hall was pulled down in 1904 to save the cost of repairs. Since then St Paul's Square has had open spaces on the north and east sides, occupied by an open-air market until Christmas 1985, after which the market moved to Horne Lane.

The appearance in the square of the 'Piazza'(1987), a refreshment kiosk, is a somewhat unusual addition. Many of the buildings surrounding St Paul's Square now look different. Although some eighteenth-century buildings remain on the south side, most are from the 1880s or later. The corner building on the right with a lantern bracket was replaced by premises built for Thompson, the printer, and later occupied by the National Provincial Bank. It now houses Ladbroke's.

Horne Lane was realigned in 1859. Rudge's viewpoint is now on the pavement behind the Civic Theatre.

15 BRADFORD RUDGE

Old Horne Lane, Bedford, as it appeared in 1835

1835. Coloured lithograph, 214 x 162 mm

Bradford Rudge made this lithograph of Horne Lane in 1835, which is the earliest date at which he is recorded as present in Bedford. Old sketch-books show that he took an early interest in drawing, tutored no doubt by his talented father, Edward Rudge, who was art master at Rugby School.

The view of Horne Lane and St Paul's Church is somewhat unfamiliar. The

church cannot be seen from this angle today because Horne Lane was diverted to the north in 1859 to accommodate the extensions to the Grammar School (now the Town Hall). The large rustic half-timbered building in the centre is the Bear Inn. The uneven tiled roof and small windows suggest an ancient building even in 1835. To the left in the background are the smoking chimneys of a house demolished with the Bear Inn when Horne Lane was re-routed in 1859.

This must have changed the rural atmosphere of this corner of St Paul's Square and created a new view of the church. The Square would be full of schoolboys by the middle of the century, many of whom would be Bradford Rudge's own pupils between 1840 and 1874.

At the time Rudge drew this picture the grand new buildings for the Commercial, or English, School (now Bedford Modern School) were nearing completion. As a newcomer Rudge seems to have taken an interest in recording the passing of the old way of life and Bedford's transition from a small rural town to a much larger, more industrial one.

Late Victorian houses in Conduit Road, west of the site of the Grey Friars (demolished 1899).

16 T.D. NEWHAM

Grey Friars' Priory, Bedford, North-West View

Date uncertain; probably copied from an original painted in 1884. Watercolour, 355 x 505 mm

The Friary Farm, which had been the Franciscan Friary before the Reformation, was a familiar Bedford building until the turn of the century. It is clearly recognisable in an old photograph of the 1890s (see Richard Wildman, *Bygone Bedford,* 1974, plate 1), though this painting is somewhat earlier and shows a large building to the left, that is, north, of the main one. Both structures were demolished in 1899. The former Friary was described as 'a large and old-fashioned building, having a deep roof and windows of the usual conventual style' by Thomas Blyth in his *History of Bedford* (1873).

The buildings were known as 'The Priory' because the eighteenth-century engravers, the brothers Buck, misnamed them, confusing them with Newnham Priory. The name 'Priory' has thus been given to a nearby street behind the present-day Safeway supermarket and the Police Station. The farm land was situated to the west of Priory Street, but the main Friary building was a little further north, nearer to Bromham Road, where there is now a small recreation ground next to Priory Lower School. At one time the lands belonging to the Friary Farm were very extensive and covered seventeen acres between Bromham Road and Midland Road.

The Franciscans, or Greyfriars, who were the followers of St Francis of Assisi, first came to England in 1224, the year in which Bedford Castle was destroyed in the siege. They had become established in Bedford by 1242, and a local benefactress, Mabel de Pateshull of Bletsoe, seems to have given them the money for a church which was consecrated in 1295. Unlike monks and canons, the friars did not at first accumulate property but lived on gifts. After the dissolution of the monasteries in 1538, the Friary buildings were used as a farmhouse. In the eighteenth century the property was part of the Earl of Ashburnham's estate. The farm was occupied in the early part of the nineteenth century by John Moore Howard, Governor of Bedford Gaol and father of John Howard, whose sons, James and Frederick, founded the Britannia Ironworks (see nos 52, 53). The Revd Timothy Matthews, an evangelical preacher, subsequently lived at the Friary Farm, and had his chapel (Christ Church) in Bromham Road nearby. The chapel has now become the Esquires Club. In the 1830s a rumour circulated about treasure being found in the grounds by some workmen who became miraculously rich, but nothing was proved. John Leland, the Tudor traveller, recorded that among the burials in the Friary church was a certain 'Queen Eleanor', but he seems to have been mistaken. While the queens of Henry II, Henry III and Edward I all bore this name, Henry II's wife was buried in France and the other two in Westminster Abbey.

In 1898 there was a spirited campaign to try to save the Friary Farm buildings from demolition. Philip Webb, the architect, and Arthur Ransom, former editor of the *Bedfordshire Times*, both wrote to William Hale White ('Mark Rutherford') in July of that year to enlist his support. Webb calls the proposal to build 'an exercise ground' 'brutal and stupid' and fears that unless the demolition is stopped 'the reputation of the town's people will be blackened for ever as an intelligent community'. Heritage was not a popular issue in Victorian Bedford, and in spite of the efforts of a few eminent people, including the Mayor, George Wells, the campaign failed. The buildings were pulled down in 1899.

Today the Friary grounds are occupied mostly by housing built in late Victorian and early Edwardian times, and the nearest place of worship is the Bedford Islamic Religious Centre.

The former Grammar School's main façade was rebuilt in 1767; an extension (*right*) was added 1859-61. The Town Hall office-block (*left*) was opened in 1963 on the site of the former Headmaster's house.

17 R.C. STRATFOLD

The Grammar School, Bedford

Dated 1827. Coloured lithograph, 178 x 222 mm

This pleasant lithograph of the old Grammar School depicts the first building of one of Bedford's famous institutions, the Bedford Charity or Harpur Trust. With its eighteenth-century statue of the sixteenth-century benefactor, Sir William Harpur, in the central niche like a saint, the Bedford Grammar School building looks much the same today, though it is now used as part of the Town Hall. The statue has been much discussed, as it is meant to portray the Bedford man, who became Lord Mayor of London and endowed the town's grammar school, as an elegant eighteenth-century gentleman. The sculptor Benjamin Palmer, not knowing what Harpur looked like, provided what he hoped was a suitable statue when the building was refurbished in 1767, as at that time it was usual to depict historical figures in contemporary dress.

Although Harpur's appearance is known only from his brass in St Paul's Church, his name must be among the most famous in the town. Born about 1496, he spent his youth in Bedford and was probably educated at the town Grammar School, then in 'Schole Lane' (now Mill Street). He left Bedford for London, became a wealthy man, and by 1533 was a freeman of the Merchant Taylors' Company. Being childless, he used his wealth to help the people of his native Bedford. By the late 1540s the old school in Schole Lane, which had belonged to Newnham Priory, had been sold, following the dissolution of the monasteries. A new school-house was needed, and Harpur acquired land in St Paul's Square to build a permanent schoolroom with a master's house next door. In 1552 Bedford Corporation obtained letters patent from Edward VI enabling it to accept an endowment, and this was the beginning of the present Harpur Trust Schools.

In 1564 Harpur bought as the school's endowment thirteen acres and three roods of land in Holborn, which is now in the heart of London, just outside the area of the City. The Mayor and Corporation of Bedford were appointed as trustees to administer the proper spending of the income from the land, and the school was to be under the supervision of New College, Oxford. Rents from Holborn paid for the schoolmasters' salaries and the upkeep of the buildings, and boys living in Bedford received a free classical education. Any surplus was to be used for marriage portions for poor girls, apprenticeships for poor boys, and alms for the needy.

Harpur was Lord Mayor of London in 1561 and was knighted by Elizabeth I in 1562. He was twice married, first to Dame Alice after whom one of the girls' schools is named, and later to Dame Margaret who is buried with him in St Paul's Church, Bedford. After his death in 1574, the endowment was administered by Bedford Corporation. The Great Fire of London in 1666 affected the price of property in the City, and building speculators, especially one Dr Barebone, became very active. Harpur's land in Holborn was leased to Barebone with whom there was legal wrangling over rents, but the rents were eventually paid and the site was developed. An Act of Parliament of 1764 created the Bedford Charity (Harpur Trust), and from that time the income to the Charity from the rents was regular and, as the whole area was built over, steadily increased. Rents from Charity properties in the 1830s were £12,000 per annum.

The school in the picture is the one built on the land in the south-west corner of St Paul's Square. Refronted in Portland stone in 1767 by Isaac Clayson of Harrold, and with 'Elizabethan' windows, the building was a landmark. A pleasant house, with a garden extending to the river, behind a wrought-iron gate was the home of the Head Master until 1892 when the Grammar School moved to the present Bedford School site. The former Head Master's house survived until 1959, when it was demolished for the building of the Town Hall office-block.

To the right is Horne Lane, as it looked before it was widened and diverted northwards to accommodate the Grammar School extensions. On the right is the Bear Inn.

18 ROCK AND CO.

Bedford Grammar School

*c.*1850s, and dated 1 June 1858, but showing proposed extensions built 1859-61. Engravings, 80 x 120 mm

Several Rock engravings exist showing Bedford Grammar School, both before and after the building of the new extension to the north. An extension became necessary as the number of pupils increased, though in the 1830s the school experienced some problems with 'insubordinate ushers, truancies and expulsions'. In the 1840s the Holborn rents (see no.17) fell because the residential population was moving out of that area of London. In spite of such financial difficulties, and the damage to the reputation of the school during the preceding decade, advertisements appeared in the press in 1843 to encourage people to come to Bedford where 'every youth whose parents have resided six weeks, receives an entirely gratuitous education at a school as good as Rugby or Harrow'. The English School, once held in the ground floor of the Grammar School building, and now called the Commercial School, was also described in glowing terms. The type of person addressed was middle class, from 'the man of fortune who happens to have a large family, or ... half-pay officers, or ... widows of Ministers, whose means may be more scanty'.

Such advertisements attracted large numbers of people who were known as 'squatters' by the local inhabitants. An

increase in the population meant large house-building programmes, and this accounts for Bedford's wealth of solid respectable Victorian housing. The influx of new families, and Bedford's growing reputation as a place where people of modest means could find a good education for their children, was undoubtedly good for the town. Dr Brereton, the Head Master from 1811 to 1855, is reputed to have been paid the enormous salary of £1,300 a year. He had taken full advantage of a change in the Harpur Trust's rules which abolished the previous limit on the number of day boys for whom he could claim a capitation fee. Thus the number of boarders declined and that of day scholars increased. From the 1840s the prosperity of the town led to the construction of many new buildings, including churches and chapels, which were financed by pious subscribers.

The Commercial School had originally been held in part of the Grammar School building, and when this school moved to new, separate premises in Angel Street (Harpur Street), the Grammar School could expand a little, but after twenty years' growth it again needed more space. James Horsford, a Bedford architect, won £50 for his design for the extension, and the building cost £6,753.2s.8d., including over £1,000 for 'preliminary law expenses' and the cost of purchasing the land and three old houses on the site. Horne Lane had to be diverted northwards, so the old houses, including the Bear Inn, were pulled down.

The opening of the extension was a very grand occasion, with flags and banners adorning the new tower, and numerous visitors. All the staff of the school were there, the Mayor and Corporation in their robes, heads of the principal families of Bedford and, of course, the scholars. Contemporary accounts note with an air of relief that 'the college representative, the Trustees and the Inhabitants' all attended amicably together, forgetting on this occasion the misunderstandings of the past, which had arisen from alleged misspending of Harpur Charity funds.

In 1892 the original Grammar School became the Town Hall, and the 1859-61 extension today houses the Mayor's Parlour and the Civic Theatre, formerly the school hall.

19 GEORGE MOORE

Bedford New Schools

Inscribed *'To the Trustees of the Bedford Charity — This View of the New Schools &c. erected by them, is, by Permission, respectfully dedicated'.*

Mid-1830s. Coloured lithograph, 290 x 413 mm

The Harpur Centre (1976) was constructed behind Edward Blore's façade (1833) for the Bedford New Schools. The street furniture dates from the late 1980s.

George Moore's skill in perspective is evident in this picture of what is today known as the Harpur Centre. To present-day Bedfordians this building is a shopping centre behind a Gothic façade, but from about 1833 to 1974 it housed a number of schools and offices belonging to the Harpur Trust.

By the 1820s the English School, which occupied part of the Grammar School building, had become very popular and crowded; elementary schools had been founded, and new buildings were essential. These buildings on the west side of Angel Street (now Harpur Street) were intended to accommodate an 'elementary' (or 'national' or 'preparatory') school, offices and living quarters for the Harpur Trust clerk, a boardroom for the Trustees, a children's home or 'Hospital' to replace one in Angel Street, which had been demolished, and the Commercial School, as the English School came to be called.

In 1830 a design by the eminent London architect Edward Blore (1787-1879) was accepted, winning £50. Moore may have based this picture on Blore's architectural drawing, since Blore himself was also an accomplished draughtsman. A preliminary plan for the English School by John Elger had been rejected, but Blore designed his new façade for Elger's plan in the Gothic style. The contract was awarded to James Tacy Wing, son of John Wing. The building cost £13,730, and the Harpur Trust was by that time overdrawn. In 1837 the Harpur complex was completed, and Moore's picture dates from about that time.

Although the Commercial School now had larger and more prestigious premises than the Grammar School, its status was lower in a society where a classical education was more gentlemanly than a practical one. The education given was useful, without concentration on the classics, and unlike the Grammar School, the masters did not have to be members of the Church of England. Since many leading townspeople were dissenters, this aspect of the school appealed to them. Teachers were in general paid less than their Grammar School counterparts, though the art master, Bradford Rudge, seems to have been an exception, perhaps because he was employed at both schools.

The Commercial School's reputation grew, however, and many pupils went on to take up 'modern' careers such as architecture and engineering.

The Elementary School was run on a monitorial system, where older pupils taught younger ones. In 1831 there was said to be 'most lamentable ignorance throughout the school', when the energetic Mr Riley was appointed as Head Master. The Elementary School moved to new premises in the Harpur complex, and by 1843 it was described as 'particularly well-conducted', though with over 100 pupils per teacher and no effective training, there still must have been immense difficulties.

Both boys and girls attended the Harpur elementary schools, but the girls' school was separate from the boys', and their education was considered less important, so less money was invested in it.

In the picture some pupils and adults can be seen in the school yard, behind a wall which was replaced by railings in 1882. Today there is a paved forecourt with lime trees and grass with some bicycle parking in front of the building. The street was cobbled in the 1830s, but it is unlikely that people sold their wares in this busy part of town, as depicted by George Moore, who has also exaggerated the width of Angel Street at this point.

20 THOMAS FISHER

Church of Saint Cuthbert, Bedford, from the North

*c.*1820. Watercolour, 223 x 267 mm

Thomas Fisher made a special project of recording important sites and buildings in Bedfordshire during the early nineteenth century. This view of old St Cuthbert's Church is from the north side, according to the sketch on which this watercolour is based. Fisher would have stood near the site of the present Linger's butcher's shop to see this view.

The small church in the picture looks completely different from the building occupying the site today. The original church is thought to have been built to serve the people living outside the eastern boundary of the early town. A new stone building was erected in the thirteenth century, the older one having been knocked down by Falkes de Breauté for his defensive works on the Castle (see no. 1). It was eventually demolished in 1845 by the Victorians, who, wishing to replace it with a more impressive building, constructed a neo-Norman church. The humble red-tiled church with few windows and thick buttresses was a Bedford landmark for centuries and is shown on all the old maps. Although despised by some as 'small and mean' and 'insignificant and ugly', the little church inspired an anonymous and rather earnest farewell poem, printed in the local newspaper in 1844, in which it is addressed:

Farewell! dear, venerable pile, farewell!
Sighs of regret shall be thy funeral knell,
Simple thy structure, not the less rever'd,
By highest, holiest, fondest thought endear'd ...

Fisher's painting suggests a country church, and indeed at the time St Cuthbert's parish had open country to the east. Along the river bank to the south-east was the hamlet of Thames Street, later Waterloo, demolished to make way for The Embankment gardens in 1889. The trees to the left were eventually cut down. The churchyard has few tombstones, and, as is typical of Fisher's pictures, there are no people. Fisher's aim was to record precisely, and in this he proves a useful source, since other artists also drew this church — in some cases very differently (see, for example, no. 21).

21 ALLEN

St. Cuthbert [*sic*] Church, Bedford

Dated 1844. Watercolour, 262 x 333 mm

It is hard to believe that Allen's picture of St Cuthbert's Church depicts the same building as Fisher's (no. 20). Allen's picture was painted in 1844, about twenty years after Fisher's, but portrays remarkably different features. It is highly probable that Allen followed a fashion for 'romantic' subjects which allowed him to alter a few details. 1844 was the year before this old church finally closed and was demolished.

This view is from the north-west, from a spot near the Georgian building at 38 Mill Street, which today houses the Citizens' Advice Bureau, with the west window visible. Allen makes the church taller and, though still small, more elegant. The wooden turret with its bell and octagonal clock are portrayed with a small weathervane on top, but the roof is made of grey slate rather than Fisher's distinctly red tiles. This suggests either that the church was re-roofed between the 1820s and 40s, or that Allen thought grey slate fitted better with a fashionably romantic perception of the church. Allen's windows are finer, and creepers and shrubs grow up the sides of the building and across the roof. There is almost a deliberate air of neglect, as if nature has been allowed to run wild around this ancient building. Two tombstones in the foreground stand like an open book, lending a romantic air and giving a sharp focal point to the picture. This composition appears to be more thought out, or perhaps contrived, than Fisher's simple document.

22 ALFRED
DE BREANSKI, JUN.

John Bunyan's home in Bedford and St. Cuthbert's Church

Early 20th century. Coloured lithograph from an oil, 176 x 298 mm

This picture of St Cuthbert's Street showing John Bunyan's house is difficult to assess, but it has been so popular that it appears as an illustration in many books on Bunyan or on Bedford and was made into a Raphael Tuck 'Oilette' postcard (textured to resemble a painting). De Breanski's picturesque scene could be either an idyllic rural vision of Bedford in the seventeenth century or its appearance at a much later date (the early nineteenth century). Looking at the clothing of figures in the picture (sometimes a helpful indicator of date), it is still not really possible to tell which century it depicts.

Nobody knows exactly what St Cuthbert's Street looked like in the 1650s when John Bunyan lived there, or even in 1838 when his house was demolished. It seems likely that the picture is an imaginative reconstruction of how the artist thought the street might have looked 250 years earlier. The first three cottages from the left are copied from a sketch by Miss L. Green which is still in existence. The sketch, signed but not dated, is thought to be *c.*1848. The cottages were demolished in 1838, so the sketch was drawn from memory about ten years later.

De Breanski's version, which is very similar to Miss Green's, was based on her sketch which was then the property of Bedford Literary and Scientific Institute and General Library. Beyond the cottages is a taller half-timbered building, different in shape from one outlined in Miss Green's sketch. This makes it difficult to decide whether de Breanski was portraying St Cuthbert's Street as it was in the nineteenth century or earlier.

Beyond the tall building is an inn with a sign outside. This is where the Ship Inn has been since at least the early eighteenth century, but the building on that site was described as a 'cottage and orchard' up until 1706. It is therefore not possible to say whether it was an inn in the 1650s. It seems probable that de Breanski inserted the Ship Inn into the picture, thereby suggesting that the view is intended to be of the 1830s, but he might have assumed that such an ancient inn could have been there in Bunyan's time.

To the right in the background is old St Cuthbert's Church. Demolished in 1845, it was rebuilt in a completely different style in 1846-7, but de Breanski would probably have seen some of the many pictures of the old church (see nos 20, 21).

Bunyan's cottage is the central one of the three. The brick-built cottage which

St Cuthbert's Street. Owing to de Breanski's odd perspective, most of these old buildings (restored *c.*1984) do not appear in the picture. The Bunyan cottage is out of the photograph to the left.

replaced it is now occupied by a chic kitchen shop with blue continental blinds, and a blue plaque on the wall records Bunyan's association with the site.

Although the picture has been considered to be inaccurate and imaginative, research reveals that it could be more accurate than was originally thought.

23 BRADFORD RUDGE

St. Cuthbert's Church

*c.*1845. Graphite with bodycolour, 220 x 275 mm

A sketch in Rudge's notebook is dated 1845 and is clearly the basis for this drawing. This, then, is about twenty years later than the picture by Fisher (no. 20) and is almost contemporary with Allen's painting (no. 21). In 1845 the old church was closed, and Rudge must have sketched it very shortly before it was pulled down, in order to commemorate it before it was replaced.

Of all the views of old St Cuthbert's Church this is perhaps the most convincing. The church is seen from the south side, with Newnham Street straight ahead and St Cuthbert's Street beyond. Rudge would have been standing near the present corner of Castle Road and Newnham Road. The church wall, though rebuilt later in the century, is still more or less in the same position, and the road is now a little wider since the houses on the right-hand side, then called Peck's Farm, have been demolished to make way for the red-brick building of St Cuthbert's Hall, built in 1892.

The church itself is clearly the same one as that portrayed by other artists. The tiled roof confirms the accuracy of Fisher's picture, but it now seems to be sagging rather badly. The wooden turret is still there, and the vestry chimney on the far side. Some of the surrounding buildings can still be seen. The house on the extreme left is the prison reformer John Howard's, at 55 Mill Street, and the Georgian building, of which the upper corner is just visible behind the west end of the church, today houses the Citizens' Advice Bureau, at 38 Mill Street.

St Cuthbert's Church.

24 BRADFORD RUDGE

St. Cuthbert's New Church, Bedford

*c.*1847. Lithograph, 256 x 302 mm

The contrast is very apparent between Rudge's charming scene in no. 23 and this picture of the new church which replaced it only a year or two later, and marks a transition from the old to the new in Victorian Bedford.

The building, designed by James Woodroffe, was erected in 1846-7 at a cost of 2,000 guineas, given mostly by local people, with a modest contribution from the rates. The style, neo-Norman, was much admired in its day, and the revival of this twelfth-century style of architecture must have looked very modern to people who had seen mainly ruins of the original style on which this is based. This somewhat unusual building was considered very fine and up to date, though certain criticisms were voiced by the Revd J. D. Parry in the *Gentleman's Magazine*, concerning the modern appearance of the roofing slate and the size of the tower, which he considered to be too large for its single bell. In calling this building 'a miniature cathedral' Parry captures its small-scale grandeur.

About twenty years after the church was built, the population for which it was intended expanded dramatically. The 300 seats provided were no longer sufficient, and F. C. Penrose, the surveyor of St Paul's Cathedral, drew up plans for 232 additional seats at a cost of £1,350. Again, the generosity of the public was depended upon, and William, 8th Duke of Bedford, was a major contributor. The north and south aisles were added in 1865, an organ chamber was built, and a porch was added to the north transept in 1907. The nave and aisles were extended westwards in 1877.

Today's church is that depicted by Rudge, with later extensions. There is a clock in the circular opening in the north transept, and the church and yard are in the middle of a traffic island around which a one-way system runs. The church was declared redundant by the Church of England in 1974, and subsequently purchased by the Harpur Trust which presented it to the Polish community. They have worshipped at St Cuthbert's since 1980, and in the late 1980s raised funds to restore its fabric, with generous assistance from Bedford Borough Council. No longer just 'St Cuthbert's', the church is now named 'The Roman Catholic Church of Sacred Heart of Jesus and St Cuthbert', St Cuthbert's name being included as a courtesy, perhaps, and a reminder of its history.

Poorly specified window guards give St Cuthbert's Church a boarded-up appearance.

25 INIGO BARLOW

The South West Prospect with the plan of St. Paul's Church and the Town Arms of Bedford

Dated 1787. Etching by I. Seago,
165 x 200 mm

Inigo Barlow's early etching of St Paul's Church is fairly accurate in all except its proportions: he makes the church resemble a huge cathedral by reducing the size of the surrounding buildings and trees. The church is seen from the south-west corner of St Paul's Square, that is, from in front of the present Town Hall.

St Paul's has traditionally been considered the first church built in the town, and some associate the site with a Saxon monastery, founded by the year 771. Certainly by 1066 there was still a group of canons attached to the church, which was mentioned in the 'Domesday Book'. Since its foundation, the church has been built, then destroyed or dismantled and rebuilt five times. This fourteenth-century church, probably larger than its predecessors, has the foundations of the earlier churches beneath it. Since the fourteenth century there have been many additions and alterations. The plan provided below the drawing indicates the shape of the north side which is not visible. The church must have looked somewhat different from the way it does today, as the north aisle was not added until 1884. Before that time it was a 'hall church', the nave and south aisle being of equal height.

The fine Georgian railings, which curve around the west end of the churchyard,

are shown in diagrammatic form. Barlow's purpose must have been to record rather than to entertain. It is probable that this picture was intended either as an illustration in a book or as a print which could be bought by gentlemen interested in the eighteenth-century pursuit of the rediscovery of charming old buildings. It is a solemn picture, and it is only to a twentieth-century eye that the tiny surrounding houses appear amusing. Though clearly not to scale, some of these may depict real buildings which surrounded St Paul's Square in the late eighteenth century.

Barlow has evidently concentrated on giving an accurate picture of the church itself. The effect is of an architectural drawing, which is emphasised by the plan provided below. The Town Arms of Bedford, from a design which dates back to the fourteenth century, show the castle and a crowned eagle.

St Paul's Church, south side. Comparison with Barlow's engraving indicates the extent of Victorian additions and alterations.

26 JOHN SUNMAN AUSTIN

St. Pauls Church, Bedford, Beds.

Inscribed *'To Charles Fred.^{k} Palgrave, Esq., Mayor, and the Town Council of the Borough of Bedford, This Plate is by permission respectfully Dedicated by their obliged & most obedient Servant, John Sunman Austin, Architect, Bedford'.*

1850. Lithograph with some tinting,
540 x 467 mm

John Sunman Austin produced and published a series of at least sixteen townscapes and illustrations of Bedfordshire churches from 1850-4. It seems that he was an unstable person with delusions of grandeur. Suffering from 'monomania' or 'vanity', he was admitted to the Lunatic Asylum for a time in 1848.

This handsome lithograph presents the confident grandeur of St Paul's in a much livelier picture than some other views of the church. It is an accepted part of Victorian Bedford. The church is shown from the east, looking towards Horne Lane. Austin's viewpoint is north of the present statue of John Howard, which was erected much later in the century. Since Barlow's picture of 1787 (no. 25), a clock has been added (1812). The church had just been re-roofed in 1849, and more restoration work was to be carried out over the next twenty years. The tower and the spire were reconstructed in 1868, and the north aisle was added in 1884. The churchyard looks much clearer of bushes and trees than it does today, and on some versions of the lithograph the name 'Walton' appears on a tombstone to the left of the gate piers. This name was probably added to the lithographic stone at a later date by someone other than the artist to commemorate a local person. The tombstone of Austin's wife, Jane, who died in 1843, can be found today in St Paul's churchyard.

St Paul's Church. Victorian interventions changed much of the detail but generally respected the overall structure.

Parts of the scene shown in the picture of St Paul's are still identifiable. On the south side of the square, to the left, Austin shows Georgian houses which were demolished in 1910 for the building of the Shire Hall extension. On the right the newly constructed Floral Hall (1849) is visible. This was pulled down in 1904 to save the cost of repairs. In the background a house that used to be to the south of the Commercial School in Harpur Street can be seen. This was demolished when Horne Lane was diverted northwards in 1859.

27 JOHN SUNMAN AUSTIN

St. Peter's Church and Green, Bedford, Beds.

Inscribed *'To the Rev. Gustavus Burnaby, M.A. Rector of St. Peter Martins, Bedford. This View is by kind permission respectfully Dedicated by his most obedient Servant, John Sumner* [sic] *Austin, Arch*t*., Bedford'.*

1852. Coloured lithograph, 482 x 699 mm

Austin again shows his skill as an artist in capturing the charm of St Peter's Green in the mid-nineteenth century. His name is twice spelt wrongly on this lithograph (as John Sumner Austin), though it is undoubtedly his work.

This unusual panoramic view, in an oval frame, seems to be seen in a camera obscura, giving a strongly Victorian feel. It spans a semicircle from The Broadway to St Peter's Street, with St Peter's Church at the centre.

The full name of the church is St Peter de Merton, sometimes wrongly spelt Martin. It is on St Peter's Green at the north end of the High Street and is thought to be a Saxon foundation, perhaps the church of the suburb outside the north gate of the early town. The church still bears fire marks said to be caused by burning during the Danish invasion of 1010. It was a much smaller church then, and the Bedford Mint might have been inside the tower. In the sixteenth century the doorway from another church, St Peter de Dunstable, which used to be on the corner of Cauldwell Street, opposite St Mary's, was transferred to St Peter's as first the west, then the south entrance. It was enclosed by a porch in 1902.

In Austin's picture the old houses that used to be on The Broadway are recognisable, notably the Stone House (not to be confused with the old Town Gaol of a similar name next to the old Guildhall). This was demolished in 1936 and replaced by Broadway House. Beyond is the end of Tavistock Street, formerly known as Offal Street, as it was the town rubbish dump, and later politely renamed Offa Street. Immediately to the west of the church is Bury Farm, an Elizabethan house, which was pulled down in the 1880s for the building of De Parys Avenue.

The church itself has been enlarged since Austin's day. It is also more obscured by trees, which may be the very ones planted in the 1830s by the Revd Philip Hunt who added embellishments such as the 'Saxon battlements' to the tower. To the east of the church is the Rectory, which was bought by the Harpur Trust in 1887 for use as school workshops and replaced by the Preparatory Department of Bedford School in 1899.

The main difference between Austin's scene and its appearance today is the size of the Green, which was slightly reduced in size when De Parys Avenue was constructed. In 1874 a statue of John Bunyan by Sir Joseph Boehm was erected at the south-west corner.

Photomontage of St Peter's Church and Green.

28 THOMAS FISHER

Saint Mary's Church, Bedford, from the S.W.

*c.*1820. Watercolour, 180 x 204 mm

St Mary's Church stands on the corner of St Mary's Street and Cardington Road, which used to be called Potter Street. Viewed from the traffic island at the end of Cauldwell Street, and looking towards the east, the scene Fisher painted is still easily recognisable. The building visible today is a combination of Norman and Perpendicular styles, with Victorian additions. The south aisle was added in 1853 at a cost of £850, but this is the only major difference.

The church is an ancient foundation. It is likely that this was the parish church of the settlement south of the bridgehead which was organised and fortified by Edward the Elder in 915, when he had the King's Ditch dug and embanked. Though not mentioned in the 'Domesday Book', the church is mentioned in the Foundation Charter of Lincoln Cathedral of 1086 as belonging to the See of Dorchester. Fairs were granted in the area of St Mary's in 1553 to supplement those north of the river, and W. H. Pyne's painting (no. 13) depicts the pig market which was held round the corner to the south of the church.

Nuns from Elstow Abbey were buried at St Mary's in the sixteenth century, after the dissolution of the monasteries, but the most famous memorial is perhaps that of Giles Thorne, the seventeenth-century parson. The Puritans suspected him of having 'Papist tendencies', and he was therefore victimised and imprisoned. He spent five years in the Fleet Prison, but at the Restoration he was appointed chaplain to Charles II. On his death in 1671 he was buried in St Mary's. His monument is 'emblazoned with his arms, and is supported by a group of female figures'. Fisher's picture, like many other examples of his work, is plain and correct and reflects the 'remarkably neat-looking edifice' described by Thomas Blyth around fifty years later. The spot must have been much quieter in the first quarter of the nineteenth century than it is now. Today heavy traffic thunders by on the A6, the main road to London, and the traffic lights and signs spoil the appearance of the west aspect of the church. In 1990 the church became Bedfordshire County Council's Archaeology Centre.

St Mary's Church from the west.

29 THOMAS FISHER

Remains of S^{t}. John's Hospital, Bedford

*c.*1820. Watercolour, 195 x 251 mm

The former St John's Hospital, which is now called St John House, is easily recognisable in Fisher's picture, viewed from the east. The front elevation facing St John's Street still has the six ogee arches on the windows added in the eighteenth century. The walls are 'plastered and whitewashed' according to notes on Fisher's preliminary sketch. In more recent times the plaster has been removed to reveal a stone wall. The lower windows have had to be protected by grilles as the shutters were removed by the Victorians.

The building has, in fact, undergone many changes since it was erected in the twelfth century. On the north side the shape is now different, though the small windows beneath the eaves are still in evidence but blocked up long ago. The Victorians added to and altered the building in 1851: the north wall was rebuilt in brick and the old chimney breast removed. Today the building probably looks more as it did in the eighteenth century. The street wall is very ancient stonework, possibly of the twelfth century, though the picture suggests it is brick.

When the Hospital was founded in about 1180 by Robert de Parys and John and Henry St John, it was a house of charity for 'needy persons free born of Bedford ... who had become poor by misfortune rather than by fault'. It was run by a Master and Brethren. From the fifteenth century the Master was also the parish's rector, the Hospital chapel having previously achieved the status of a parish church. In the seventeenth century, during the Commonwealth, the Town Council who had the advowson or power to appoint the rector, appointed John Gifford (see no. 30) to the position, as they were Puritans and supported his views. At that time Gifford's Independent Church needed a meeting-place, and his appointment as Rector of St John's enabled his followers to be based there. Gifford lived in the Rectory, which had once been the Hospital. John Bunyan spent many hours discussing his faith here with 'holy Mr Gifford' whom it is said he later depicted as 'the Interpreter' in *The Pilgrim's Progress.*

Bedfordshire County Council acquired the building in the mid-1960s and commissioned its extensive restoration to the designs of John Gedge, undoing much of the damage inflicted by the Victorians.

It is now leased by the County Council to St John Ambulance, who moved there in 1970. The St John's Hospital estate was wound up by an Act of Parliament in 1881, and the proceeds of the sale of its farmland for building paid for Bedford Park, opened in 1888.

St John House.

30 THOMAS FISHER

S^{t}. John's Church, Bedford

*c.*1820. Watercolour, 284 x 205 mm

The present church was not erected until early in the fourteenth century and shows signs of an extensive restoration carried out in 1869-70. It is remarkable how similar Fisher's painting is to the church's present appearance: many features are recognisable, though the refurbishment of the lower windows is evident. The Agnus Dei statue, put into the niche on the west wall in 1869-70, was carved by Harry Hems of Exeter. The only part that looks very different is to the left where the south side of St John's Hospital is visible. The old appearance of the Hospital, from the other side, can be seen in Fisher's companion watercolour (no. 29). John Gifford, a Commonwealth Rector of St John's, was a remarkable man. He is said to have been wild in his youth, a major in the Cavalier army who somehow escaped execution after taking part in the Second Civil War of 1648. He came to Bedford in disguise and set up as a doctor, continuing to indulge in his old habits of 'drunkenness, gambling, swearing and all kinds of immorality'. Eventually, after a period of great stress, he underwent a conversion. His newfound zeal led him to seek out a group of religious people he had offended, and after being for a time mistrusted, he was accepted and allowed to preach, ultimately becoming their pastor.

John Bunyan (see nos 22 and 31) was attracted to the church which met at St John's. It was a Congregational or Independent church whose members believed that a church should consist of converted Christians only, and should not be bound by the regulations of any outside body, only by what was found in the Scriptures. Bunyan had also had a disturbed youth and through Gifford's help he came to have confidence in his acceptance by God.

St John's Church from the south-west.

31 THOMAS FISHER

Mr. Bunyans Meeting House Bedford & the Vestry in which his chair is preserved

*c.*1820. Watercolour, 202 x 247 mm

This painting by Fisher shows the back (the south side) of the three-gabled brick meeting-house as it looked in about 1820. It was later enlarged and refurbished. This Old or Great Meeting was pulled down in 1849 as it had by then become 'prejudicial to the health and comfort of the hearers and the Minister'. The site was used for the much larger and grander building which stands there today, Bunyan Meeting.

Bunyan Meeting, south side.

John Bunyan is Bedford's most famous son. Born in 1628, he was brought up in Elstow, where his father had a forge. The family was poor, but they may have paid for John to learn to read and write at a local school. In his youth he revelled in 'being filled with all unrighteousness', and his troubled conscience produced dreams 'about evil spirits in monstrous shapes and forms', but 'the mad youth rushed on in his career of sin'.

For a time Bunyan was probably in the Parliamentary army and found himself among people who discussed new ideas in religion and politics, but he appears to have returned to Elstow as undisciplined as when he left. Here he married his first wife in about 1649. By 1653 he was becoming increasingly concerned about his salvation and, seeing his life as wholly sinful, undertook to reform his ways. 'Our neighbours ... did marvel much to see such great and famous alteration in my life and manners', he declared. He was drawn towards a group of earnest folk, members of the Bedford Independent Church, led by John Gifford (see nos 29 and 30).

In 1655 Bunyan was ready to tell others of his deeply felt and hard-won faith. The same year he and his wife moved to St Cuthbert's Street, Bedford. Soon afterwards his wife died and he remarried in 1659. His second wife was called Elizabeth. By the time of the Restoration in 1660 Gifford was dead and Bunyan was one of the leaders of the Bedford Independent Church, but with the return of the monarchy an Anglican rector was reinstated at St John's and Bunyan and his friends had to find a new meeting-place. His preaching was now against the law, and he was imprisoned on several occasions in the County Gaol in Silver Street, though tradition incorrectly puts him in the Town Gaol under the eastern side of the old Town Bridge. It is in gaol that he is said to have had the famous dream that inspired his greatest work, *The Pilgrim's Progess,* published in 1678.After their expulsion from St John's, the church members met in private houses and later acquired a barn in Mill Street for their meeting-house. It was not until 1707, nearly twenty years after Bunyan's death in 1688, that a new meeting-house was erected on the site of the barn at a cost of £400.

32 JOHN SUNMAN AUSTIN

Bunyans Meeting, Bedford, Beds.

Inscribed *'This Plate is respectfully submitted to the Public in Memory of the Revered name of John Bunyan, by their most Obedient Servant, John Sunman Austin Architect Bedford. This chapel was erected in the Year of Our Lord 1849 at a Cost of £4200 Raised by Voluntary Contributions. Built on the Site of the Original Meeting bearing Date 1650'.*

1854. Tinted lithograph, 335 x 355 mm

Austin's lithograph of 1854, which shows the new Bunyan Meeting when it was just four years old, is 'respectfully submitted to the Public in Memory of the Revered name of John Bunyan', in the hope that copies would be bought by the townspeople. Austin notes that the 'Original Meeting' dated from 1650. He refers here to Gifford's church, as the barn that stood on this site was used by Bunyan's congregation only after 1672. He still calls himself an 'Architect', though it appears that he did not practise this profession seriously.

The architects of the new Meeting were James Tacy Wing, son of John Wing (see no. 4), and Thomas Jobson Jackson, County Surveyor. The builders were Messrs Berrill, Maxey and Ward, who used mostly red brick and limestone. This fine Victorian building in the style of James Gibbs, who was considered to be the best classical architect since Sir Christopher Wren, still looks very much the same, except for a porch built on to the front to protect the bronze doors depicting scenes from *The Pilgrim's Progress*. Designed by Frederick Thrupp, the doors were donated by the 9th Duke of Bedford in 1876. Renovations in 1974 have not changed the building's external appearance.

The building originally cost about £4,200, which was raised by voluntary contributions. Its opening on 20 February 1850 was an occasion of great splendour. People arrived from all over the country, many by train from London, the railway link to Bletchley having been opened only four years previously. They listened to the Revd Dr Harris's sermon on the theme of 'the alleviation of suffering' and afterwards attended a 'collation' at the Bedford Rooms in Angel Street (now the Harpur Suite in Harpur Street).

Austin's picture shows many of the buildings surrounding the new Bunyan Meeting. The Castle Rooms and the Higgins Brewery, now occupied by the Cecil Higgins Art Gallery and Bedford Museum respectively, are hidden today by the Bunyan Meeting Sunday School building of 1866, designed by John Usher. In the far distance the tower of St Mary's Church, south of the river, is just discernible between the Brewery buildings. Further west, on Mill Street, are some sheds belonging to a timber yard,

Bunyan Meeting by James Tacy Wing and Thomas Jobson Jackson.

which were replaced by modern offices in 1972, and 45-47 Mill Street, which are still there. Beyond the houses the famous roof with the golden ball on top can be seen. This belongs to the original building of the Howard Chapel (no. 33), enlarged at the same time as the Bunyan Meeting was rebuilt.

Howard Chapel as enlarged by John Usher in 1849. From 1971 it fell into disuse and was burnt out in 1985.

33 JOHN SUNMAN AUSTIN

Howard Chapel, Bedford, Beds.

Inscribed *'This Plate is respectfully submitted to the Public in Memory of the Founder, John Howard, the Philanthropist, by their most Obedient Servant, John Sunman Austin, Architect, Bedford. This chapel was Enlarged by voluntary contributions in the Year of Our Lord 1849'.*

1854. Lithograph, 380 x 280 mm

It is very sad that the Howard Chapel stands today as a skeleton of its former self. Once it was one of the grand and imposing buildings of Mill Street, which were celebrated in an old rhyme quoted by John Hamson in *Bedford Town and Townsmen* (1896):

The three ridges, the round ball,
The magpie's hop and the beggars' call.

The 'three ridges' were the roof of the old Bunyan Meeting; the 'round ball' (or 'golden ball' in other versions of the rhyme) was on top of the New Meeting, the original name of the Howard Chapel; the 'magpie's hop' referred to a caged bird near the entrance to the Mill Street Baptist Chapel, where unyielding Baptists went following the appointment of a Congregationalist minister at Bunyan Meeting; and the 'beggars' call' referred to the followers of the Revd Timothy Matthews, an enthusiastic field preacher of the early nineteenth century who summoned worshippers, mostly poor people, with a trumpet.

The New Meeting was founded in 1773 by people who broke away from Bunyan Meeting in response to 'a change of sentiment which took place in the minister of the Old Meeting ... with respect to the ceremony of baptism ...'. John Howard, the future prison reformer and philanthropist, had up to this time been a member of Bunyan Meeting. He was in no way an extremist but helped to provide funds for a group wishing to dissociate themselves from the minister and a number of members of Bunyan Meeting who were insisting on adult baptism, with which many disagreed and which went against the comprehensive tradition of that congregation.

A building was designed by Daniel Millard and erected in 1774 on the present site. It is said that materials from an old barrage in the river, demolished in 1770, were used in the foundations. A watercolour of *c.*1820 by Thomas Fisher shows a charming brick-built chapel standing back from the street with the famous ball on top of its roof.

By 1847 the congregation had grown and the chapel needed enlarging and refronting. John Usher, a well-known Bedford architect, was commissioned, and by 1849 the work was completed. The new front brought the entrance nearer to the street. Seen from a raised position, maybe from a building opposite, the impressive new chapel celebrated in this lithograph incorporates the old building and bears an inscription on the façade: Erected MDCCLXXIV – Howard Chapel – Enlarged MDCCCXLIX.

Next door to the chapel beyond the graveyard was a large half-timbered building which was demolished later in the nineteenth century. Offices have since been erected on the site. In November 1865 the Revd W. Alliot wrote: 'The memorial [to John Howard] at Bedford [the Howard Chapel] is in a dilapidated condition, and requires immediate restoration at a cost of about £1,000'. The funds were raised quickly by local benefactors and internal refurbishments were duly carried out. In 1866 the chapel was reopened to the admiration of all. Now a ruin damaged by a fire in 1985, the chapel has been disused since 1971.

The building has a place in the history of planning legislation, owing to a decision by the Law Lords in 1975 that a chapel listed as a building of architectural or historic interest may not be demolished without planning permission. This decision followed legal action taken by Bedfordshire County Council.

34 THOMAS FISHER

Moravian Chapel, Bedford

*c.*1820. Watercolour, 173 x 187 mm

The first Moravians, or United Brethren, came to Bedford in about 1742. Originally they were religious refugees from Moravia, which was part of what is now Czechoslovakia. They came to England at the instigation of their protector and leader, Count Zinzendorf. The early followers of the Moravians influenced people in Bedford who were already affected by the Evangelical movements centred on Oxford and Cambridge, and by Wesley's disciples. By 1745 a follower called Mrs Okely had provided them with a meeting-place in the High Street, and within six years their numbers had grown sufficiently to allow them to acquire land in St Peter's Street. Here they built their chapel and 'choir houses' for the Single Brothers and Single Sisters, with a burial-ground behind. Nearby there were rented houses for the Married Brothers and Sisters. The congregation's own buildings still stand today, though the chapel was entirely rebuilt in 1864-5.

Fisher's sketch for the watercolour is annotated 'of good red brick' describing the building material. It is a plain building with large windows and is similar in style to other chapels of the period in the Bedford area – for example the old Meeting (no. 31) and the original Howard Chapel (no. 33). It was finished in 1751 and was paid for by donations from local Moravian members. Next door to the chapel to the west (left) is the Single Sisters' House, built in the same year, and to the east, not visible, there was a house for Ministers or Labourers. Moravians had a particular interest in providing education for the children of their members. During the eighteenth century several unsuccessful attempts were made

St Luke's United Reformed and Moravian Church by James Horsford (1864-5).

to set up boys' schools. A more successful girls' school, founded in 1802, survived until 1914.

Fisher's painting is unadorned and lacks any characterful or colourful features, but since he always took pains to be precise, it is likely that the chapel was exactly as it is shown here.

35 BRADFORD RUDGE

Chapel & Ladies School &c. of the United Brethren, Bedford

*c.*1850. Lithograph, 297 x 389 mm

This unusual 'aerial' view of the north side of St Peter's Street was commissioned by the Moravian congregation (see no. 34) and drawn and lithographed by Bradford Rudge in 1851.

The row of buildings in the foreground is still recognisable, even though the second building from the left, the Moravian Chapel (now called St Luke's United Reformed and Moravian Church), was rebuilt by the architect James Horsford in 1864-5. Pilasters and pediments had been added to the doorways of the original simple building before 1851. The Single Sisters' House, which is the first building on the left of the chapel, was built in 1751. In the eighteenth century the Single Sisters, or unmarried Moravian women, had to support themselves by lace-making, the local industry. They were also 'engaged in embroidery and tambour work'. The brothers Lysons reported that nearly forty women lived there in 1806. This house was converted into flats in 1991-2.

The house on the other side of the chapel was that of the Minister. The large house set back to the far right with extensive grounds was also the property of the Moravians and had at one time been used by the Single Brothers, and briefly as a boys' school. The artist James Gillray was a pupil here. In 1851 it housed a very successful Ladies' College, founded originally in 1802, which was a girls' boarding-school attended by pupils not only from Bedford but from all the surrounding counties. The row of houses in the centre dates from the mid-1840s.

The gardens at the back are now part of the Bedford School estate.. On the left in the background it is possible to see the tower of St Peter's Church, which Rudge has 'moved' a considerable distance to the east in order to include it in his picture. Behind the Moravian buildings are a burial-ground and gardens. Beyond are the open fields of what was then rural Bedford.

Nowadays an aerial view would reveal in the far distance Bedford Park, the Robinson Pool, the Cemetery and Brickhill to the far left beyond De Parys Avenue. To the right Bedford School stands in the background with its many buildings. The Harpur Trust purchased the former Moravian Ladies' College in 1921 for the use of Bedford School. Renamed the Howard Building, after Geoffrey Howard, a former Chairman of the Trust, it was extended westward in a sympathetic style by Sir Albert Richardson in 1961-2. A new building, named after another Chairman, Sir Maurice Craig, was built parallel with the Howard Building, between it and the St Peter's Street frontage in 1935, so the Howard Building is no longer visible from the street.

35 BRADFORD RUDGE

Chapel & Ladies School &c. of the United Brethren, Bedford

36 THOMAS FISHER

The Methodist Meeting in Angel Street, Bedford

*c.*1820. Watercolour, 184 x 220 mm

John Wesley, the famous preacher, first came to Bedford in 1753, and made thirty-two visits in all. A tireless evangelist who would preach in all weathers and in any spot that was convenient, Wesley recognised that Bedford had a strong tradition for dissent and gained a considerable following in the town. In the early days he would preach all day on St Peter's Green. He observed in 1757: 'There is no cursing and swearing in the streets, no work done on the Lord's Day. Indeed there is no open wickedness of any kind now to be seen in Bedford.' Alderman Parker, one of his followers, offered a corn loft in Angel Street for the use of the preacher, but people remarked that 'the stench from the swine under the room was scarce supportable'. Wesley and the Bedford congregation supported it until a 'new room' was built in 1763.

By the early nineteenth century the number of Methodists had increased and a new building was needed. The chapel seen in Thomas Fisher's watercolour was erected in 1804 and was the first built specifically for the Bedford Methodists. It stood on the site of the present Bedford Central Library and the extension to Beale's department store in Harpur Street, then known as Angel Street. This is presumably the site of Alderman Parker's corn loft. The building was a modest red-brick Georgian-style hall with two storeys, a central doorway and a low wall with railings. A circular plaque was inscribed 'The Methodist Chapel 1804'. The chapel was regularly extended until it became necessary to rebuild it completely in 1832 to accommodate 'the multitudes who flocked to hear'. The congregation swelled from forty-five in the 1780s to 108 in 1804 and to more than 750 in the 1830s, and the leader of the flock, Mr William Cumberland, commented that 'we are getting on famously at Bedford'.

The cottage to the left was demolished when the new chapel was built in 1832, but the Minister's red-brick house on the right remained until a schoolroom was built on the site in 1883.

Below St Luke's United Reformed and Moravian Church by James Horsford (1864-5) and earlier Moravian buildings.

Right The Methodist Meeting stood on the site now occupied by part of Beale's store and the Central Library.

The Harpur Suite (former General Library, then Public Library 1936-72), built in 1834 as the Bedford Assembly Rooms.

37 BRADFORD RUDGE

Wesleyan Methodist Chapel with Ministers House, and the Bedfordshire General Library

*c.*1840. Lithograph, 344 x 550 mm

From 1840 Rudge worked very near to the site where he drew this picture and must have walked past these buildings every day. Seen from the front of the new buildings of the Bedford English School, this print is nearly contemporary with George Moore's picture of the schools (see no. 19), which shows the view directly opposite. Like Moore, Rudge has made Harpur Street (then known as Angel Street) and its buildings seem wider, grander and more spacious than they really are. The school wall was replaced by railings in 1882, but Edward Blore's gate-piers remained until 1974.

The Methodist or Wesleyan Chapel replaces the older chapel seen in Fisher's picture (no. 36) and was built in 1832 slightly to the east of the older building. Methodism was becoming increasingly popular in early nineteenth-century Bedford, and the congregation continued to grow. In 1842 the chapel was enlarged.

Other buildings visible are the Minister's House, a double-fronted Georgian house (almost in the centre), demolished in 1883, and the Bedford Rooms, a Greek Revival building with four Doric columns. Built in 1834 and paid for by public subscription, this grand and rather unprovincial edifice, no doubt considered very fashionable at the time, still stands, with extensions, and is called the Harpur Suite. Like other buildings in this style, it stands out distinctively from its surroundings. However, Rudge has failed to draw the portico in its correct proportions. Known as the Bedford Assembly Rooms in Rudge's time, it was used as a public ballroom and a gathering-place for special events in the town, such as the 'collation' at the opening of the new Bunyan Meeting in 1850 (see no. 32). Later in the nineteenth century it was taken over by the Bedford General Library, a private lending and reference library. In 1936 it became Bedford's first Public Library. When the new Central Library was built on the site of the Methodist Chapel in 1969-72, the old building was converted into the Harpur Suite, which is today used as a meeting-room for the Bedford Borough Council and is available for hire by any organisation. Thus it has become the 'Assembly Rooms' once more. The rooms directly under the portico are the offices of the Council's Amenities Department. The house beyond it to the right still stands facing St Paul's Square, but its garden was used in 1899 for new offices, which now blend in well with the older-style buildings.

38 THOMAS FISHER

High Street, Bedford
Entitled 'Street View, Bedford'

*c.*1820. Pencil sketch, 199 x 372 mm

Fisher's sketch of the High Street looking south is remarkable in its painstaking detail and includes helpful coded annotations such as 'RB' (red brick?), 'DRB' (dark red brick?) and 'C' (cream?). It is not known whether he produced a watercolour based on this sketch, since none has survived, but his notes to remind him of colours suggest that he probably did. An old photograph of the 1860s reveals that by that date little had changed except for the replacement of the building above where the donkey is standing on the right-hand side.

Today most of the buildings on the east side are adapted or refronted versions of those that were there in the 1860s, but several of those in the sketch, particularly towards the south of the street, have been either rebuilt or refurbished to make a more regular alignment of façades. The attractive Georgian porticoes and spacious shop windows of this elegant street were similar to Woburn today, but most have now been replaced with modern doorways and plate glass. No. 35 High Street can be seen to the left of the man in the cart, south of the gable-end. In this building John Howard, the agricultural implement-maker (see no. 52), was to sell his goods from 1835 onwards. It may have been built originally as the Barley Mow Inn, and after Howard's time it became the premises of Bacchus, then Gibbs and Dandy, all ironmongers. A cut-price emporium called 'Poundsaver' today occupies the building.

St Mary's Church is just visible at the end of the street, though it is now mostly obscured by the Moat House Hotel, which is 'a tower block plonked down with breathtaking insensitivity' according to an article in *The Times* by Nigel Andrew (5 August 1989). The Georgian house with the elaborate portico on the left is now Curry's store, the modern shop-front occupying about a third of the height of the building.

On the west (right) side the most attractive buildings, a seventeenth-century shop and the archway leading to the Old George Inn, have gone. The handsome premises at 42-44 High Street, which were mistakenly identified by the Revd C. F. Farrar, grandson of John Howard the ironfounder, as a Court House, are recognisable by their three oriel and three dormer windows. This building was probably medieval with seventeenth-century alterations. In the 1860s it was T.T. Gray, wine merchant, and the architect John Usher had offices above the shop. By the late nineteenth century it was Sell and Willshaw's fish shop, but the front retained its original style despite alterations to the ground floor. Pulled down in 1964, it was replaced by modern shop buildings in an undistinguished style. The central oriel window was saved for the town through the efforts of F. W. Kuhlicke, then Director of Bedford Museum. It is possible that the three fine oriel windows originally belonged to the Market House which was built in the middle of the High Street in 1682-4 and finally demolished in 1780, but as no reliable pictorial record of that building survives, this cannot be proved.

High Street. St Mary's Church tower is just visible to the right of the insensitively sited Moat House Hotel.

39 THOMAS FISHER

Bedford County Jail

*c.*1820. Watercolour, from an interleaved copy of Lysons' *Bedfordshire* (1806), 220 x 318 mm

Before this gaol was built, the County Gaol was on the north corner of the junction of Silver Street and High Street, and it was the place where John Bunyan (see no. 31) was imprisoned for his nonconformity in the seventeenth century. The old building was rat-infested, insanitary and dilapidated. John Howard (see no. 33), former High Sheriff of Bedfordshire, published *The State of the Prisons* in 1777, which stirred the public conscience, and by the 1780s plans were being made for a new gaol, possibly in the High Street. Land could not be obtained, however, so the gaol was eventually built in 1801 in St Loyes.

Described either as a 'strong and handsome building' (Blyth) or 'dull and gloomy' (Matthiason), depending on the writer's point of view, it was designed and erected by John Wing and included the luxury of baths. It is likely that Wing's progressive design was influenced by the pioneering work of George Dance the Younger, who had designed Newgate Prison, London, in 1769. The same 'chains on iron rings' motif (in the form of an 'M') which symbolised the bonds by which the criminal was restrained, appears above the entrance in both designs. A humane attitude towards criminals, which had been current for some years, was now being translated into a practical application, and Howard's work of 1777 emphasised these points at the time when Bedford County Gaol (or 'Jail' as it was then spelt) was being planned. Originally prisoners slept in separate rooms, or at most two to a cell.

J. H. Matthiason wrote in 1831:

> Immediately over the entrance is a high square turret of stone containing the turnkey's chambers, and on the top having a flat roof, surrounded with iron palings, on which is erected the Drop for the execution of criminals, whenever those wretched and disgusting exhibitions are appointed to take place ...

He was himself soon to experience the unpleasantness of a spell in gaol for debt, as was another artist, John Sunman Austin. Matthiason's horror at public executions might have been considered oversensitive in an age when one could be given a death sentence for relatively minor crimes, or be transported to the colonies. Until 1822 it was still possible to hang for the theft of 12d. Rural people were desperately poor in the early nineteenth century, and theft was a common crime. Other crimes for which people were imprisoned were assault, poaching and even body-snatching, when fresh corpses commanded a high price at medical schools.

Though the new gaol was more humane than the old one in providing 'every thing for the bodily comforts of its inmates that humanity, joined with propriety, can suggest', life there could still be hard and miserable. In spite of improved conditions there were still typhus epidemics, and the punishments consisted of 'carrying large balls of lead, or ... turning a handle a certain number of times every day'. Occupations at the prison were oakum-picking and mat-making for men, and lace- and strawplait-making for women. However, life was not always bad, and for some inmates it might have been better than outside, with plum pudding at Christmas. One governor, John Moore Howard, grandfather of the Britannia Works Howards (see nos 52, 53), tried an 'open prison' system in the early nineteenth century, allowing prisoners to work on his land. The justices, however, disapproved of this and dismissed him in 1814.

A House of Correction was built in 1819 behind the prison to replace an old one in Cauldwell Street. The inmates were not so much hardened criminals as nuisances sent to prison for 'bastardy, lewdness and light offences'. Behaviour problems led to the installation in 1821 of a corn-grinding treadmill to tire the energetic prisoners sufficiently to prevent outbreaks of disorder. This building was later demolished as conditions were found to be worse than those in the main prison.

The present main entrance and flanking lodges date from 1849, but parts of the old County Gaol still stand in the centre of Bedford Prison in St Loyes, where problems of overcrowding are more serious today than at any time in the long history of the prison. A large extension on the east side of the prison was completed in 1992.

Her Majesty's Prison.

40 THOMAS FISHER

Sessions House & Town Hall, Bedford

*c.*1820. Watercolour, 201 x 242 mm

This watercolour by Fisher shows one of the buildings which used to stand on the site of the present Shire Hall on the south side of St Paul's Square. It was called the Sessions House and was built in 1753 as its Georgian style suggests. John, 4th Duke of Bedford, gave 500 guineas towards its building. Fisher tended to be a documentary artist, and the building must in reality have been the 'little squat Georgian Shire Hall' that the Revd C. F. Farrar describes. In 1831 J. H. Matthiason called it 'a neat-looking stone building' and commented that it was small and overcrowded.

The building had a variety of uses, as well as being the place in which the Assizes, Quarter Sessions, Petty Sessions and County Court were held. When the old Guildhall was demolished in 1806 as a result of the Bedford Improvement Act, the Borough Council met there too (hence 'Town Hall'). During 1815, before the completion of the Preparatory School in Angel Street (now Harpur Street), the Harpur Trust was given permission by the magistrates to use the Sessions House for classes until their school was ready. While the old Bunyan Meeting was being rebuilt (see nos 31, 32), it was even used as a temporary place of worship for a few months.

The building retained its function as the Sessions House and Town Hall until the

Shire Hall by Alfred Waterhouse (1879-81).

late 1870s when it was demolished to make way for a splendid new Victorian building designed by Alfred Waterhouse and erected in 1879-81. The new Shire Hall is in red brick and terracotta with a Gothic porch, Elizabethan windows and pavilion roofs, and is much larger than the building it replaced. Other buildings on the south side of the Square were also demolished to make way for Victorian and Edwardian improvements, thus changing the scale of that part of the Square and giving it a monumental and more urban appearance.

The Sessions House is one of the few major Bedford buildings, demolished in the age of photography, of which no photograph is known to exist. The Town Council was soon to acquire its own premises when Bedford Grammar School moved out of St Paul's Square in 1892, leaving its original buildings to become what is now the Old Town Hall and Civic Theatre (see no. 18). Apart from court functions, the new Shire Hall was well placed to serve as offices for the newly created Bedfordshire County Council in 1889, and remained as such until the present County Hall was opened in 1969. The Shire Hall is now used as Magistrates' Courts and ancillary offices.

41 ARTIST UNKNOWN

Bedford Town Election

Dated 1835 but believed to depict the election of 1832. Oil on canvas, 618 x 755 mm

The Swan Inn features in this lively scene of the Bedford Town Election. Although this picture has been known for many years as the Election of 1835, it seems likely that it in fact depicts the election of 1832. It is dated 1835 in the bottom right-hand corner, but the slogans on the election banners suggest that the issues under discussion were those of 1832. Recent cleaning of the picture has revealed that the figure '5' seems to be an alteration.

The anonymous artist, depicting a prominent political event, must have been aware of which event he was recording for posterity. It is not possible to confuse the issues of 1832 and 1835, though the candidates were the same in each year. Samuel Crawley and William Henry Whitbread were the Whig candidates in both years, and Captain Frederick Polhill was the Tory candidate.

Whig banners, in the yard of the Whig stronghold, the Swan, proclaim 'Freedom to the Slave', 'Whitbread and Reform'. Crawley's main platform was for the abolition of slavery which was achieved in 1834, and by August of that year the *Northampton Mercury* reported that Bibles were being sent to 'emancipated slaves in the sugar colonies'. Slavery would therefore no longer have been an issue by 1835, and banners for that year would have borne different slogans. In 1832 the Reform Act was passed ensuring fairer representation of the electorate through a redistribution of parliamentary seats. Whitbread's support for this newly introduced Act (the election took place in December 1832) is shown by the slogans of his followers, which figure prominently in the foreground. This evidence seems to indicate conclusively that the picture refers to that year rather than to 1835. Polhill's Tory followers assert traditional adherence to the old order, with 'King, Lords and Commons', 'Throne and Constitution', and 'Church and State' on their banners, surrounding their headquarters, the George Inn on the left.

The confusion over which election is depicted may arise from the fact that the picture was for a long time the property of the Conservative Club. They would naturally interpret the scene as a Tory victory. The Tories did win one of the two Borough seats in the 1835 Election, with Polhill polling 490 votes to Crawley's 403 and Whitbread's 383. They had, however, lost the 1832 Election to the Whigs, Crawley beating Polhill by just three votes (Crawley 486, Polhill 483), and Whitbread winning outright with 599 votes. Polhill took his defeat badly and accused Crawley of bribing would-be supporters

with free drinks. Polhill himself was not above this underhand and relatively normal practice; tokens for pints of beer at the Ship Inn for 'Captain Polhill's Friends' were printed and distributed. These may have 'encouraged' support, culminating in the 1835 victory. Polhill's petition was heard in 1833, but Crawley kept his seat. Forty-two electors were struck off the register as a result of Polhill's complaints.

The Swan Hotel by Henry Holland, a minor masterpiece in an eroded setting.

42 THOMAS FISHER

Bedford Infirmary

*c.*1820. Watercolour, 211 x 278 mm

This solitary Georgian building that seems far from civilization is in fact the old Bedford Infirmary between Kempston Road and Ampthill Road, seen from the Ampthill Road side. When it was built in 1803 this was on the very edge of town, since it was considered wise to remove the sick from society. Fisher's remote-looking building seems to be on a raised bank above the level of the road. J. H. Matthiason remarked in 1831 that it 'commands the traveller's notice at a considerable distance in approaching the town'. Other contemporary pictures look more attractive and less forbidding than Fisher's, and show pleasant grounds with lawns and trees.

Built in 1801-3 by John Wing, the Infirmary was financed by subscribers, who according to the amount of their subscription were allowed to nominate an appropriate number of out-patients or in-patients. Private individuals contributed varying amounts, as did churches and parishes on behalf of those in their care. The Whitbread family made a generous contribution of £8,000 to the initial cost of building and upkeep, but the average contribution of supporters was two guineas a year. Bazaars and other fund-raising events were also held, for there was no form of public health care, except in the hated Union Workhouses.

Since the professions of medicine and

nursing were in their infancy, the staff of the hospital were not at first trained nor always successful in their treatments. The hospital seems to have been very basically furnished at first without even the provision of seats in the waiting-room. Medical books were donated, however, and the Infirmary possessed an extensive medical library. Although until the nineteenth century it was not considered a very gentlemanly profession, hospital medicine was gradually acquiring respectability, and the availability of textbooks would have aided young doctors learning their trade by practice. Eventually the profession came to be regulated, and qualifying examinations were introduced.

The site today is raised slightly above road level, but this is the only feature in which it resembles the old site. Now on a very busy main road, the new hospital, rebuilt from 1895 onwards, is much more extensive.

43 JOHN SUNMAN AUSTIN

Infirmary and Fever Hospital, Bedford, Beds.

Inscribed '*His Grace the Duke of Bedford, K.G., Grand Visitor: William Henry Whitbread, Esq., President. The Institution was founded in 1803, by the munificent Gift of £9,236, through the spirited liberality of the late Samuel Whitbread, Esq., M.P.; and in 1826, Enlarged by the liberal Gift of £2000 by the Marquis of Tavistock, & other Donors: also in 1847, the Fever Hospital was added, to the honour of the Town & County, by Voluntary Subscribers, To whom this Drawing is respectfully submitted by their most obedient Servant*, JOHN SUNMAN AUSTIN, ARCHITECT BEDFORD'.

Dated 1850. Lithograph and watercolour, 492 x 670 mm

By the 1850s the new Fever Hospital had been built (completed 1848), again by public subscription. Austin dedicates this lithograph to the subscribers. Various enlargements had been made to the main building, notably in 1826 with a gift of £2,000 from the Marquis of Tavistock. Seen again from the Ampthill Road, the site seems much less remote and less raised up than in Fisher's picture (no. 42). Still a rural location, with cattle grazing nearby, the scene is much livelier.

The Fever Hospital would have been an isolation wing for the treatment of people with contagious diseases. Advertising for the Harpur Trust Schools in 1843 assured prospective parents that the air of Bedford was 'salubrious', and in 1831 J. H. Matthiason had said that 'its water in general is naturally pure and wholesome'. This was not strictly true, since there were cholera epidemics and the Fever Hospital was completed in time to receive its victims in a severe epidemic of 1849. 'Consumption' (tuberculosis) was common, and although Matthiason praised Bedford's water, as a social observer he could not fail to recognise the conditions in which the poor of Bedford lived and worked. He describes the Well Street area (Midland Road) where 'the operative classes ... confined in close courts and low houses, and toiling at their lace pillows ... inhale an atmosphere unchanged by the salutary breezes of the streets; and entail sickness and disease on themselves'. He abhors 'the pestiferous practice of packing crowds together in obscure and unventilated corners' as this undoubtedly led to the spread of disease. Scarlet fever and typhus were relatively common, and even leprosy was not unknown in nineteenth-century Bedford.

Considered old-fashioned by the end of the century, this pleasant-looking hospital was replaced with more modern buildings, today known as Bedford General Hospital (South Wing). Bedford's other hospital, North Wing, in Kimbolton Road, is centred around the old Union Workhouse building.

Bedford General Hospital (South Wing) from Kempston Road.

43 JOHN SUNMAN AUSTIN *Infirmary and Fever Hospital, Bedford, Beds.*

44 THOMAS FISHER

The Lunatic Asylum, Bedford

c.1820. Pencil sketch, 169 x 241 mm

This pencil sketch was probably Fisher's preliminary drawing for a watercolour. This exists but its present whereabouts are unknown.

Until the early nineteenth century most people suffering from mental illness were cared for by their parish or family. A few were sent away to asylums in larger towns, such as Bethlehem Hospital (Bedlam) in London, where they underwent treatment which was rudimentary, experimental and sometimes cruel. There were also private asylums for the better off. Mental illness and handicap were feared and misunderstood, and few effective humane treatments had been discovered.

In 1808 the Lunacy Act was passed, permitting counties to spend rate money on building their own asylums, and Bedfordshire was a pioneering county in building one of the earliest. Samuel Whitbread headed a committee which resolved to build a modern asylum on the Ampthill Road, near to the Infirmary. Completed by John Wing in 1812, at a cost of £9,584, the building was considered 'well-arranged, excellently ventilated and furnished with every convenience'. It nevertheless had bars on the windows, 'presenting the revolting idea of confinement' according to J. H. Matthiason in 1831. Male patients were housed on the right and females on the left, each with their own room, with an administration area in the middle. A young couple was appointed as Keeper and Matron at a joint salary of sixty guineas a year.

Although Bedford had shown a progressive attitude in providing a 'fine-looking' building in extensive grounds, treatment at the asylum was undoubtedly still primitive. Strait-jackets, wristlocks and handcuffs were still the means of restraining violent patients in an age when psychotherapy and the use of drugs were unknown. By the 1850s, however, a more humane attitude was displayed in the 'Manual of Duties of Ward Staff' where it was emphasized that kindness and pity were necessary in the treatment of lunatics who were not responsible for their actions.

From 1845 onwards all counties were expected to make provision for the treatment and care of lunatics. If they did not build their own asylum, they had to make arrangements for patients to go to another county. Hertfordshire and Huntingdonshire began to send patients to Bedford, so the premises had to be enlarged. Extensions were added to Bedford Asylum in 1850, so that it would be able to accommodate about 250 patients. The Commissioners in Lunacy suggested improvements and alterations. The county of Bedford paid £4,000 for the work, and Hertfordshire contributed £350 towards new kitchens.

Less than fifty years after the opening of the asylum, it was regarded as 'unsuitable for the modern ameliorative treatment of insanity' and was replaced by the Three Counties Asylum (now known as Fairfield Hospital) at Arlesey. The old asylum was pulled down and the land used for housing. The former burial-ground became the site of a playground.

45 FREDERICK GARNER

The Embankment

Dated 1886. Oil on canvas, 250 x 358 mm

Frederick Garner's oil-painting of 1886 is one of a pair, the other being a picture of Newnham Bridge.

This shady, leafy scene looks strangely unlike a view from the same spot a century later. At the time this picture was painted The Embankment had recently been laid out. A new road ran along the river, and paths were made for riverside walks. Previously the area had been known as Thames Street, Thames-side or Waterloo (Waterloo Road perpetuates the name) and was one of the more picturesque but dilapidated areas of the town, with old damp houses by the river's edge. As The Embankment was being developed, a subscription was raised to buy and pull down these poor dwellings in 1889, with the help of a donation of £500 from the 9th Duke of Bedford. In 1894 the 11th Duke gave the nearby Russell Park to the town as an area for recreation.

The new middle classes who were coming to the town so that their children could attend the Harpur Trust Schools did not want to live near a slum. Large houses were built, set well back from the river. Paths along the river's edge were constructed and trees planted at regular intervals along the banks. Horse-chestnuts were planted near the Town Bridge end of the river walk, and weeping willows nearer to Russell Park, which was landscaped after 1894 (see no. 10). The banks were still grassy then, and the river itself contained more reeds and other plants than it does today.

Garner's picture suggests that there were water-lilies growing in the river. This is probably the stretch leading to Newnham Pool which had been a favourite spot for courting couples in the mid-nineteenth century. The flower-beds which are now to be seen on The Embankment as far as Bushmead Avenue were laid out soon after this picture was painted and give the area a more urban look.

Facing page
Aerial photograph from the north, 1992.

The Suspension Bridge by John J. Webster (opened 1888).

46 HENRY BURN

Bedford from the North

*c.*1850-5. Coloured lithograph, 391 x 578 mm

Burn's view of Bedford from a location which was probably in the present cemetery gives an idyllic and picturesque scene of rural pursuits in a country setting not far from the small town. The picture dates from before the cemetery was laid out in 1855 on land formerly belonging to Mr Whitbread, and the whole extent of the town can clearly be seen across an open vista of fields. Landscape photography was at this time becoming popular, and its influence is evident in this scene.

From left to right many buildings and landmarks can be identified. The area behind Waterloo is in the east (on the extreme left), then come St Cuthbert's and St Peter's Churches. The new Bunyan Meeting in Mill Street and the Old Corn Exchange, or Floral Hall, in St Paul's Square (both completed in 1850, helping to date the picture) can also be seen. St Paul's Church with St John's Church behind it and the Methodist Meeting in Angel Street in front are visible near the centre. It is possible to make out Edward Blore's new English School (see no. 19), also in Angel Street, then the roof of the Penitentiary in Offa Street and the tower of Holy Trinity Church in The Crescent in the west.

Today this vista is obscured by the tall shady trees of the Cemetery and Bedford Park, opened in 1888. If it were possible to see the panoramic view beyond the trees, many landmarks would still be recognisable. Bedford School playing-fields and Victorian housing around Park Avenue, Kimbolton Road, Goldington Road and The Embankment to the east and Black Tom to the west would alter the appearance to some extent.

46 HENRY BURN

Bedford from the North.

See also colour illustration on page 10.

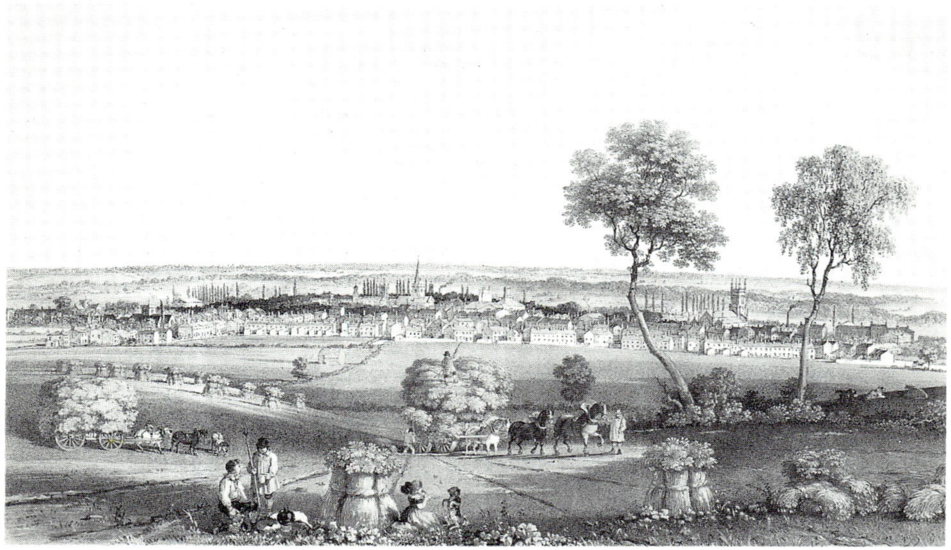

47 LILIAN STANNARD

An Old Herbaceous Garden, Castle Close, Bedford

*c.*1901. Coloured lithograph cut from an unidentified magazine, based on an original watercolour, 240 x 352 mm

The date of this print is uncertain but is likely to be before the summer of 1901 when Lilian Stannard married Dr Walter Silas and moved to London. She did not return to Bedford to live until 1919 but probably visited often during the intervening period. In 1901 Castle Close was the home of the Higgins family, whose brewery and family house are still there. They had leased the site from the Dukes of Bedford for many years, but it was not until 1908 that they finally bought it. Until 1908 Lawrence Higgins, Cecil's bachelor brother and a keen amateur gardener, lived there. The brewery is now occupied by Bedford Museum, and the family house by the Cecil Higgins Art Gallery. The grounds are the site of Bedford Castle which was demolished in the thirteenth century (see no. 1).

The part of the garden depicted cannot be identified with certainty. The wall at the end may be the one which runs along Newnham Road, so the path would run along the south side of the present lawn in front of the house, with the mound to the right and The Embankment and river beyond.

Edwardian English garden paintings, of which this is a splendid example, portray the idyllic, abundant and peaceful atmosphere of the era. A garden like this gives the feeling that summer will never end.

48 LT.-COL. GEORGE OLIVER RYBOT

18-26 Kimbolton Road

After 1872. Watercolour, 190 x 263 mm

Though sent to England for his education, George Oliver Rybot's home was in India until his retirement at forty-five in 1872. He enjoyed sketching local views there and was interested in fortifications and civilian architecture. On his return to England he settled in Bedford in the 1870s and was living at Harpur Villas, Harpur Street, in 1877. By then he had four children, three of whom were under five, and this may be the reason why he chose to retire to Bedford where a good, cheap education could be had at the Harpur Trust Schools. In this he was typical of many ex-army newcomers to the town who came to be known as 'squatters' by local Bedfordians, somewhat resentful of the interlopers' taking advantage of their schools. Rybot continued his interest in drawing and painting and shows himself in this charming watercolour of Kimbolton Road to be a gifted amateur artist.

This painting of nos 18-26 Kimbolton Road is remarkable for its accuracy. The same buildings can be seen today from St Peter's Car Park, which the patch of greenery has now become. The only major difference is that the stucco-fronted houses have been repainted and the trees are larger. The first house on the left, no. 18, is now grey and white with black window frames, while the large building next to it, nos 20 and 22, is now cream and white. The trellis for climbing plants has been removed, and a hedge has grown up in front. The large tree which now stands in the road may well be a mature version of the small tree in front of no. 22. Nos 24 and 26 are also virtually unchanged except for an elegant bay window which has been added on the south wall at first-floor level. These houses are now painted white on the front.

Kimbolton Road has been a fashionable address in Bedford ever since it was built in the early 1840s as a speculative development by the Woodroffe family of builders. Long before the laying-out of St Peter's Car Park in the early 1960s, the grassy area shown by Rybot had been a tennis court. During the Second World War an American Officers' Club was established there in prefabricated concrete huts, later used as offices and stores by the Ministry of Health.

Today this part of Kimbolton Road forms part of a very busy gyratory system taking traffic on to the A428 Cambridge road. The rural appearance has now completely departed.

18-26 Kimbolton Road.

2-6 Goldington Road.

49 LT.-COL. GEORGE OLIVER RYBOT

2-6 Goldington Road

After 1872. Watercolour, 191 x 266 mm

This is another delightful watercolour by Lt.-Col. Rybot (see no. 48), and must have been painted from a window on the south side of the road between the junction of St Peter's Street and The Grove. The modern location is the other half of the gyratory system which Goldington Road/Kimbolton Road junction has become. This is now a busy part of the main road (A428) to and from Cambridge.

The large building on the left, nos 2-4 Goldington Road, is still in existence, and although recognisable, some alterations have taken place. The high chimneys are now lower, and the stucco walls have been painted cream and beige. The columned arcade remains the same, but much of no. 2 is obscured by a tall hedge and a large shrub of which the beginnings seem to be visible in Lt.-Col. Rybot's painting. The luxuriant trees which were there a century ago have gone, and a car park now occupies the spot where there was once a garden.

Today no. 2 is used as doctors' surgeries, whilst no. 4, next door, is divided into offices. The greenhouse belonging to no. 4 was pulled down a long time ago. No. 6 on the far right was the architect John Usher's house, called 'Hiawatha' after Longfellow's fashionable poem, and built in 1867, so it was quite a modern house when Rybot painted it. In the foreground there seems to be a garden wall in front of 'Hiawatha', with trees and bushes; this too disappeared when the house was demolished in 1968, and a large office-block (Zurich House) now occupies the site.

Today the spire of St Paul's Church is obscured by the Municipal Offices (opened in 1963), but the trees planted for the Queen's Silver Jubilee in 1977 are good equivalents of those existing in 1851.

50 ARTIST UNKNOWN

Bedford Regatta, 1851

1851. Oil on canvas, 568 x 768 mm

This large and colourful oil-painting was donated to the Corporation of Bedford by Councillor W. H. Chetham in 1927. Chetham's family were Bedford boat-builders and suppliers, and had their own wharf. Chetham's grandfather and possibly other members of the family are shown in the picture, but individuals cannot be identified. The anonymous artist may have been a keen rower, as the scene is drawn from a boat in the middle of the river. The charming naïvety of the picture suggests that he was an amateur artist.

The Great Ouse has always been used for leisure pursuits, such as boating and fishing. Informal regattas took place during Victorian times, one of the earliest being in 1848, which was reported in the press because of an accident to a child spectator who, eager to view the boats from the Town Bridge, collided with a horse and cart. The event was formalised in 1853, the year of the first official Regatta. This picture, which is dated 1851, the year of the Great Exhibition, depicts one of the less-organized regattas, not so much a formal race as a mêlée of boats out for pleasure, though by that date it had obviously become a very popular occasion.

The landmarks are easily recognisable as St Paul's Church spire on the left, the Swan Inn and Town Bridge to the right of centre, and Nash's Maltings on the far right. If one looks at the same view from near County Hall today, much has changed. St Paul's spire is almost entirely obscured by tall buildings along the north bank of the river. Nash's Maltings have gone, and St Mary's Gardens are now on the site. Set back from that site is Mander College.

THE OUSE REGATTA, SKETCHED FROM THE GARDENS OF THE SWAN AT BEDFORD.

51 ARTIST UNKNOWN

The Ouse Regatta

From *The Illustrated Times,* dated 31 August 1861. Wood engraving, probably after a drawing by Edward Hull (1823-1905), 150 x 230 mm

This newspaper cutting gives a different perspective of the Regatta from the well-known oil-painting (no. 50). Seen from the east side of the Town Bridge this time, the picture gives more emphasis to the spectators than to the competitors. A contemporary account on the reverse describes the grand dinner at the Swan, celebrating victories, awarding prizes and drinking toasts.

It is likely that this wood engraving is based on a drawing by the well-known Bedfordshire artist Edward Hull (1823-1905), who was working for *The Illustrated Times* between 1859 and 1861. This scene of a boat race is viewed from the Swan Gardens behind the Swan Hotel on the north bank. St Paul's Church is in the background. The Gardens are very full, many visitors having come for the day on excursion trains. By this time travelling by train was quite usual, as Bedford had had a railway station at St John's since 1846 and at Midland Road since 1859. The bands of the Bedfordshire Militia and the Bedford Rifle Volunteers play near the bowling-green, and a variety of flags flutter in the breeze. Silver cups for the winners presented by Messrs John Bull, silversmiths, then of High Street, are set out for all to admire on a table in front of the bands.

Today The Embankment (see no. 45) is a busy road running along the north bank of the river. Plans for its construction were begun in the late 1860s, and the Swan Gardens were eventually removed *c.*1870 to make way for a new road, running from the north end of the bridge, along the river about two-thirds of a mile to Newnham Bridge. People still come to Bedford to admire the Ouse in its picturesque setting, and the Bedford Regatta is still held in summer, attracting competitors from all over Britain and from other parts of the world.

The Embankment. Construction began *c.*1870.

52 ARTIST UNKNOWN

The Britannia Ironworks at Bedford

From an unidentified newspaper, dated 14 July 1860. Coloured wood engraving, 86 x 356 mm

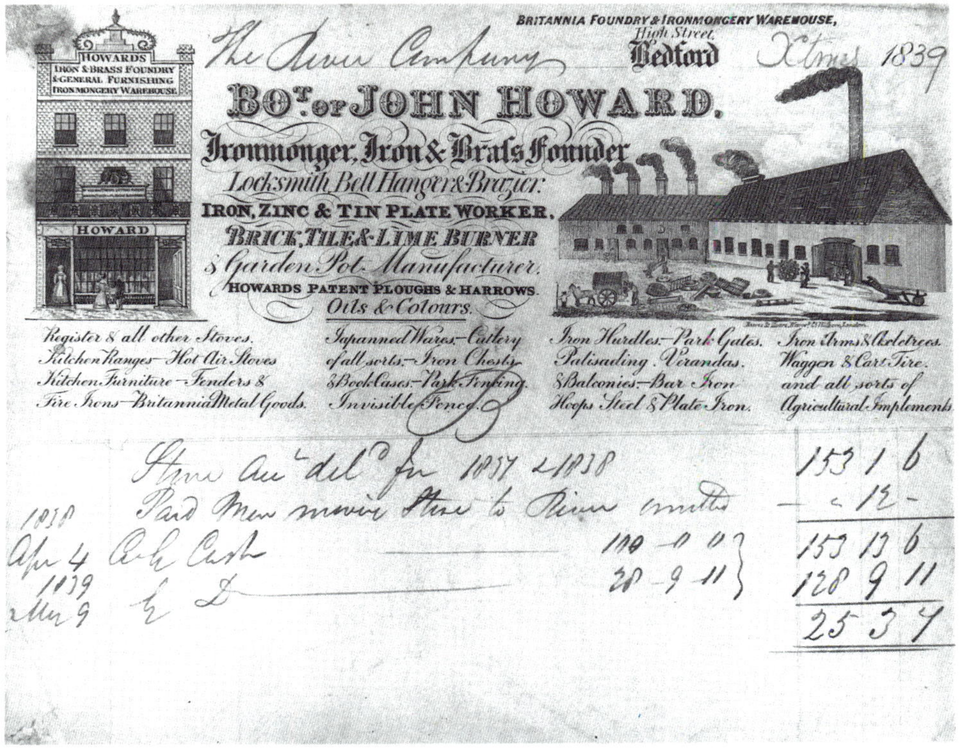

ARTIST UNKNOWN

Howard billhead

1839. Wood engraving, 189 x 231 mm

The newspaper cutting of 1860 is one of the earliest pictures of the Britannia Works, which were built less than a year before. The printer evidently did not intend this simple wood-engraving to be preserved for posterity, or he would have been more careful to align the letters in the title. The artist has drawn the site from the south-east side, making it look more extensive than it is in reality.

The factory was the pride of Victorian Bedford. In an entrepreneurial age this was 'the most complete agricultural implement manufactory in the world'. A prestigious London architect, Robert Palgrave of Pall Mall, who also happened to be the nephew of a local chemist and former Mayor, designed the works. He confidently placed a very grand gateway at the entrance, which prompted a contemporary journal to comment that it resembled 'the portal to some sybaritic Castle of Indolence or some luxurious palace of learning'.

The Howard brothers, who built the works, took over the management of their father's business in 1851, the year in which the Howard plough won a prize medal at the Great Exhibition. John Howard, father of James and Frederick, but no relation to Bedford's eighteenth-century prison reformer of the same name, was educated at the Bedford Commercial School, and subsequently took up an apprenticeship at

Olney, sponsored by the Harpur Trust. He learned the ironmongery business thoroughly and eventually bought a shop in Bedford at 35 High Street, which was later the premises of Messrs Bacchus (see no. 38). Behind the shop was Bedford's first purpose-built iron foundry, which has now been demolished. In its place is a derelict-looking car park. Howard sold a great variety of items, including 'invisible fences'. A bill of sale of 1839 shows the earliest Howard works and the shop, with elegant shoppers outside.

Agricultural implements became an important part of Howard's trade, and his sons became interested in designing new and more efficient ploughs with which they began to win prizes. By the time they took over the works Howard's ploughs were already well known. Eight years later, at a cost of £35,000, the sons purchased land on Cauldwell Priory Estate and built their modern factory, part of which still stands today.

The road in the foreground is Kempston Road, and the roof of the Crown public house, which still exists, can be seen bottom left. The gateway looks very much as it does today, and to its left are the main administrative offices where the Howard brothers worked, with statues of Britannia and Ceres on top, denoting patriotism and their indirect debt to the goddess of corn. These offices also still exist behind newer buildings. The main part of the foundry, the five rows of buildings parallel to the road, was demolished in the late 1960s, but the despatch bay to the right behind some trees still exists in an extended form.

53 ARTIST UNKNOWN

Britannia Works from the North Side

Early 1860s. Coloured lithograph,
457 x 1230 mm

This anonymous lithograph used to hang in one of the offices of the Howard brothers, James and Frederick. Two identical lithographs were commissioned, one for each brother. One is in the Bedford Museum and the other is in the Board Room at George Fischer Castings, which now occupies the Britannia Works on Kempston Road.

In the right foreground the River Ouse can be seen with boats carrying goods to

Britannia Ironworks' entrance gateway (built 1859).

and from the wharves at the back of the works. A busy railway with locomotives pouring forth clouds of steam is visible on the left. The Britannia Works had its own railway track to carry raw materials and parts from one workshop to another. This modern production-line technique was ahead of its time in the 1860s.

Beyond the buildings, on the south side, the large Italianate gate stands grandly at the entrance on Kempston Road. Behind the gate was a modern factory with contented, if disciplined, workers The despatch bay to the right of the gate as the premises are entered from the south appears to be longer in this picture than it was in the newspaper cutting of 1860 (no. 52), but shorter than in an impressionistic and rather inaccurate picture of 1864 celebrating General Garibaldi's visit to the works, which had by then achieved international renown. The despatch bay was used for checking out completed goods, but it was also where the Howard brothers delivered numerous sermons to the workers on the virtues of honest toil. In the 1860s the Britannia Works employed 600 men and produced 10,000 finished components annually. Extensions were built to designs by John Usher in the 1870s.

James Howard was a progressive employer. 'I like the system of piece-work', he said in a lecture delivered at the Working Men's Institute, Bedford, 'as it enables the workmen to earn higher wages, and the master pays for no more and no less than is done'. On the subject of overtime he said: '[I] have invariably found as a result of overtime, continued for any lengthened period, a large number of men on the sick list. I believe if men work ten hours a day, they will do more in a year than if worked twelve hours.' The hours seem long to us, though they were not excessive by Victorian standards. The thinking behind these words made economic sense to the Howard's and the factory was efficient and prosperous. Exports were sent all over the world, and the Britannia Works produced many prize-winning designs, such as their celebrated steam-ploughs (see no. 52). Trains carried away 300 trucks per month laden with Howard's products from their own private goods station on a line connected to the Midland and London and North Western Railways in the 1860s. Goods were also carried by river to King's Lynn and Wisbech, and places beyond.

The factory was so famous that news of it travelled worldwide, and in the late 1860s Prince Satsuma of Kagoshima, Japan, 'honoured them by an inspection'. In just over a century it is ironic that it is now the British who look with respect and wonder upon Japanese manufacturing technique.

54 BRADFORD RUDGE

The Bedford Times

Inscribed *'This print of the Bedford Times coach is respectfully dedicated by permission to William Henry Whitbread Esq*[re]*, by his most obedient & obliged servant J. Matthew Crispin'.*

c.1846. Coloured lithograph, 402 x 550 mm.

This lively scene, a favourite of many Bedfordians, depicts the departure of the famous Bedford Times Coach for London from outside the Swan Inn. The travellers in the picture have traditionally been regarded as portraits of well-known townspeople, though some of these identifications have been disputed. According to one 'key', from left to right, starting with the coachman, they are said to be: George Crow, whip in hand and wearing a blue jacket; behind him Lawyer Rogers, chatting to Mr Tucker, both suitably clothed in travelling coats. Mr Williams of the firm Sanders and Williams, Agricultural Implement Makers, meanwhile secures his luggage on top of the coach, while the portly Alderman Fyshe Palmer settles into his rather exposed perch at the back. The Revd Thomas Sier, later Vicar of Ravensden, stands by the rear wheel of the coach and Mr Charles Higgins, jun., sensibly ties a handkerchief over his face in preparation for the clouds of dust that will fly as the coach speeds along bumpy unpaved roads to London. Squire George Peter Livius, JP, who lived at a splendid house in large grounds on the corner of St Cuthbert's Street and Goldington Road, waits for the departure of the coach in his smart grey frock-coat and hat. The gentleman in a dark blue coat is the Rt. Hon. Lord Ongley of Old Warden, who appears to be travelling with a servant who stands beside him. Under the portico of the inn fishmonger Lilley earns some extra cash as a porter and heaves a heavy trunk towards the coach. Charles Higgins, sen., landlord of the Swan Inn, oversees the departure of his son, Charles jun., and the guests from the doorway, relaxing with his hands behind his back and wearing red carpet slippers. J. Serjeant, the head ostler, attends to the horses. According to another 'key', Mr Williams stands by the wheel and the Revd Sier wears the dark blue coat, with Charles Higgins, jun., standing between him and Squire Livius. Lord Ongley stands in front of the left-hand column in this version, which identifies neither the man on the coach roof nor the one tying on the handkerchief.

The Bedford Times coach made its first journey in 1825 and was one of many running between Bedford and London via Hitchin or Luton. There were also long-distance coaches passing through Bedford, such as the Peveril of the Peak, the Leeds Mail, the Nottingham Rapid, the Kettering Coach, the Eagle and the Wonder. The Bedford Times was noted for its good time-keeping: it used to leave at 8.30 a.m. and return from London at 8.30 p.m. each evening, and on one occasion was dug out of snow three times before it arrived at Shefford. It normally arrived at the Blue Boar Inn, Holborn, by 1 p.m. A clock which used to be carried on the coach may now be seen at the Cecil Higgins Art Gallery.

When the London and North Western Railway station was opened at St John's, Bedford, on 18 November 1846, coach travel became too slow and uncomfortable, and these conveyances ceased to run, probably to the relief of many who had travelled in them.

The George Inn, visible behind the wall, was converted into Murkett's Garage in 1910, which occupied the site until the present Swan Court was erected in 1959-60. An article in *The Times* on 5 August 1989 describes Swan Court as 'a low-level oblong block, entirely undistinguished'. Otherwise the Swan looks much the same with its balconied Ionic portico. The South African War Memorial statue (1904) now stands in the forecourt near the spot where a porter heaves a basket.

The forecourt of the Swan Hotel could be a memorable space, but the confusion of materials makes the present layout very unsatisfactory.

BIOGRAPHIES OF ARTISTS AND PRINTERS

Works included in this book are indicated after the biographies

ALLEN

First name not known, fl. 1840s

Possibly a local watercolour artist but not well known.

St. Cuthbert [sic] *Church, Bedford* (dated 1844)

ARNALD, GEORGE

1766-1841

Landscape painter. Born of a modest rural family in Farndish, Bedfordshire, Arnald showed an early interest in art and was encouraged by a local patron possibly the Revd Thomas Orlebar Marsh. Became a pupil of William Pether in London and exhibited at the Royal Academy from 1788. Contributed illustrations to *The Beauties of England and Wales* (1801) by John Britton and Edward Wedlake Brayley. In the early 1800s his patrons were Sir Thomas Bernard, Mr Herbert (whose Killarney estate Arnald visited), Lord Carnarvon (from 1809) and Sir George Beaumont. Later patrons were the Countess of Bridgewater, the Earl of Portsmouth and the Duke of Gloucester.

An album containing watercolours and drawings of Bedfordshire village scenes, together with reminiscences (some in rhyming couplets), compiled by George Arnald in the 1830s, was purchased at auction by Bedfordshire County Record Office in October 1990.

Elected to the Royal Academy as an Associate Member in 1810, though he was never to become a full member. Awarded a £500 prize for *The Battle of the Nile* (now at Greenwich Hospital) in 1825. Published *Picturesque Scenery on the Meuse* in 1835 and *A Practical Treatise on Landscape Painting in Oil* in 1839.

Both his son and daughter were also artists.

The Demolition of Old Bedford Bridge, built 1224 (dated 1812)

AUSTIN, JOHN SUNMAN

1806 or 1808-60

Born in London, but living in Bedford *c.*1832-56, after which he moved to Oxford where he died on 7 December 1860. Married Jane Kimmon (d. 1843). Carpenter, builder, lithographer and self-styled architect; claimed to have worked with William Wilkins, architect of King's College, Cambridge (though no record of this appears to exist), and said to have collaborated on a plan for the Harpur Trust Infants' School with James Horsford, 1841, but no other architectural work known. Treated at Bedford Lunatic Asylum 1848. Imprisoned for debt 1846-7 and 1853.

Unsuccessfully applied for post of County Surveyor, Bedford, 1854. His son, William Frederick Kimmon Austin (1834-99), was also an artist and engraver of topographical views, particularly of Norfolk and the River Thames. 'John S. Austin & Son' published a lithograph of the Martyrs' Memorial, Oxford, in the style of John Sunman Austin's views of Bedford.

St. Pauls Church, Bedford, Beds. (1850), *Infirmary and Fever Hospital, Bedford, Beds.* (dated 1850), *St. Peter's Church and Green, Bedford, Beds.* (1852), *Bunyans Meeting, Bedford, Beds.* (1854), *Howard*

Chapel, Bedford, Beds. (1854)

BARLOW, INIGO
Fl. *c.*1780s-90s

Produced illustrations for Rees's *Encyclopedia*, a portrait of Mrs Siddons as Rosalind and plates for *The Dramatic Works of Shakespeare* and Irlande's *Hogarth*.

The South West Prospect with the plan of St. Paul's Church and the Town Arms of Bedford (dated 1787)

BURN, HENRY
Fl. 1830s-50s

Painter and engraver living in London. Exhibited at the Royal Academy in 1830.

Bedford from the North (*c.*1850-5)

CARTER, JOHN
1748-1817

Architectural draughtsman. Born in Ireland. From 1768 made drawings for Henry Holland the Elder. From 1774 to 1786 drew for *The Builders' Magazine*. Published several books and architectural and antiquarian drawings, wrote two operas, and published works on Gothic architecture. Made an important drawing of Hereford Cathedral's Mappa Mundi showing it displayed at the centre of a triptych in the 1780s. From 1798 wrote 'Pursuits of Architectural Innovation' for *The Gentleman's Magazine*. Exhibited at the Royal Academy between 1781 and 1794. Twenty-eight folio volumes of sketches sold at Sotheby's in 1818 for £1,695.

George Inn Yard (dated 1783)

DE BREANSKI, ALFRED, JUN.
Fl. 1893-1945

Popular painter of late nineteenth and early twentieth centuries, son of Alfred de Breanski, sen. Some paintings were used in the Raphael Tuck 'Oilette' series of postcards.

John Bunyan's home in Bedford and St. Cuthbert's Church (early 20th century)

FISHER, THOMAS
1782-1836

Amateur artist who worked from 1816 as Searcher of Records at the East India Company, London. Keen interest in the 'unspoiled' buildings of Bedfordshire and visited the county regularly between 1812 and 1822, staying at Felmersham with the Marsh family. Commissioned to paint watercolours of Battlesden Park. Produced numerous watercolours of Bedfordshire buildings, and drawings of architectural and antiquarian subjects. Exhibited at the Royal Academy in 1804 and 1806.

Bedford Castle – now a Bowling green, St. Paul's Church and New Market Place, Church of Saint Cuthbert, Bedford, from the North, Saint Mary's Church, Bedford from the S.W., Remains of St. John's Hospital, Bedford, St. John's Church, Bedford, Mr. Bunyans Meeting House Bedford & the Vestry in which his chair is preserved, Moravian Chapel, Bedford, The Methodist Meeting in Angel Street, Bedford, High Street, Bedford, Bedford County Jail, Sessions House & Town Hall, Bedford, Bedford Infirmary, The Lunatic Asylum, Bedford. (all *c.*1820)

FRASER, ROBERT W.
1848-1906

Popular landscape artist from a well-known family of prolific Bedford artists. Educated at Bedford Grammar School. Exhibited at the Royal Academy between 1876 and 1892.

Old Duck Mill (1885)

GARNER, FREDERICK
Fl. 1880s

A local amateur artist. Painted in oils. His highly 'atmospheric' pictures are characterised by careful attention to natural forms and the effects of sunlight.

The Embankment (dated 1886)

HAVELL, ROBERT, JUN.
1793-1878

Engraver of topographical views and military, sporting, coaching and natural history subjects, of 79 Newman Street, Oxford Street. Son of Robert Havell, sen. Best-known work was Audubon's *Birds of America*. Engraved J. H. Matthiason's *Bedford Bridge with Swan Inn and Gardens* (dated 1824).

HOGG, ALEXANDER
Fl. *c.*1790s

Publisher of prints of 16 Paternoster Row, London. Published engravings by George Noble, including *Bedford Bridge* (1790s).

HULLMANDEL, CHARLES JOSEPH
1789-1850

Draughtsman and lithographer, mostly of landscapes and topographical views. Son of a German musician. An early pioneer in lithography technique. Printed George Moore's *Bedford New Schools* (mid-1830s), and R. C. Stratfold's *The Grammar School, Bedford* for *Select Illustrations, Historical and Topographical, of Bedfordshire* by the Revd J. D. Parry, 1827.

JACKSON, THOMAS JOBSON
1820-94

Architect and artist. Lived in Bedford from about 1846. Partner of James Tacy Wing. County Surveyor of Bedfordshire 1854-8. Served on Bedfordshire County Council for three years from 1889. Alderman and magistrate. Designed extensions to the County Gaol, layout of Bedford Cemetery, new Bunyan Meeting (with James Tacy Wing), police stations at Luton and Ampthill, farm buildings for the Whitbread family and restoration of St Mary's Church, Bedford, and Elstow Church. Known as 'a champion of the deserving poor' in his role as Member of the Board of Guardians of St Mary's parish.

Mill Meadow (1879), *Early morning on the Bedford Ouse* (1889)

MADELY
Fl. 1840s

Printer of 3 Wellington Street, Strand. Printed Bradford Rudge's *The Bedford Times* (*c.*1846).

MATTHIASON, J. H.
Fl. *c.*1820s-30s)

Mathematics master at the English, or Commercial, School (now Bedford Modern School) from *c.*1821. Amateur artist and writer. Published *Bedford and Its Environs* in 1831. Imprisoned for legal debts incurred when he unsuccessfully sued his employers, the Harpur Trust, for wrongful dismissal. He had been dismissed for being 'deficient in earnestness and zeal'. In prison continued to be troublesome to the authorities but was supported by visits from friends. Believed still living *c.*1850.

Bedford Bridge with Swan Inn and Gardens (dated 1824)

MOORE, GEORGE BELTON
1805-75

Landscape and architectural painter. Pupil of Augustus Charles Pugin (1762-1832), who was a draughtsman in the office of John Nash and specialised in perspective drawings of 'Gothic' houses. Moore was later a teacher of drawing at the Royal Military Academy, Woolwich, and at University College, London. Wrote on the theories of perspective and colour: *Perspective, Its Principles and Practice* (1850) and *The Principles of Colour applied to the Decorative Art* (1851). Exhibited at the Royal Academy between 1830 and 1870.

Bedford New Schools (mid-1830s)

NEWHAM, T. D.
Fl. 1880s

Watercolour painter.

Grey Friars' Priory, Bedford, North-West View (date uncertain; probably copied from an original painted in 1884)

NOBLE, GEORGE

Fl. 1795-1806

Engraver. Known to have been working between 1795 and 1806 but may have been working considerably earlier since his *Bedford Bridge* depicts a view as seen before 1765. Made engravings for Hume's *History of England* and Boydell's *Shakespeare*; also engraved portraits.

Bedford Bridge (1790s)

PYNE, WILLIAM HENRY

1769-1843

Studied with Henry Pars (1734-1806), the watercolourist, at Pars's School, probably in the 1780s. Founder member of the Society of Painters in Water Colour, but resigned in 1809. Exhibited at the Royal Academy between 1790 and 1815. Specialised in rural subjects, which included figures and animals. Also painted portraits. Published *The Microcosm of London* (1803) and *The Costume of Great Britain* (1808). Together with the publisher Ackermann he published *History of the Royal Residences* (1819). He later produced literary works of anecdote and gossip and edited *The Somerset House Gazette*. He died poor and unhappy.

The Pig market in the yard of the Fountain Inn, Bedford, with St. Mary's Church in the background, (dated 1806), *Bedford Bridge from the South East* (c.1807)

ROCK AND CO.

Fl. 1850s-70s

Engravers of popular prints for mass production. Specialised in small topographical picture-books of well-known places such as churches and public buildings in England, sometimes using a picture by a well-known artist as a model. Also published caricature books and panoramas.

Bedford Grammar School (c.1850s and 1858)

RUDGE, BRADFORD

1813-85

Landscape painter. Born in Coventry, son of Edward Rudge (1789-1841), also an artist, who taught at Rugby School. Bradford Rudge came to Bedford in about 1835 and made lithographs and paintings of local scenes. Also painted scenes in North Wales and Surrey. By 1837, resident in Offa Street (now Tavistock Street) and later at 'Leahurst', 8 Goldington Road, Bedford. In 1840 appointed art master at Bedford Commercial (or English) School and Bedford Grammar School. Exhibited at the Royal Academy 1840 to 1883. Honorary Secretary and local agent for the Art Union of London in 1847.

Old Horne Lane, Bedford, as it appeared in 1835 (1835), *Wesleyan Methodist Chapel with Ministers House, and the Bedfordshire General Library* (c. 1840), *St Cuthbert's Church* (c. 1845), *The Bedford Times* (c. 1846), *St. Cuthbert's New Church, Bedford* (c.1847), *Chapel & Ladies School &c. of the United Brethren, Bedford* (c.1850)

RYBOT, LT.-COL. GEORGE OLIVER

1827-1912

Born in Mhow, India, of an army family. Served in the Bengal Artillery c.1851-67. Awarded a medal in the Indian Mutiny Campaign (1857). Retired to England in 1872, and came to Bedford soon after. Sketched Indian scenes while in Bengal and continued this hobby in England on his retirement. Some sketches of India are held by the National Army Museum.

18-26 Kimbolton Road, 2-6 Goldington Road (both after 1872)

SEAGO, I

Fl. 1780s

Print seller and engraver of High Street, St Giles, London. Engraved *The South West Prospect with the plan of St. Paul's Church and the Town Arms of Bedford* (dated 1787) by Inigo Barlow.

STANNARD, LILIAN

1877-1944

Born at Woburn. Daughter of Henry John Stannard and sister of Henry Sylvester Stannard. Came from a family of well-known artists. Lived in Bedford 1877-1901, then in London and Sussex. Specialised in garden pictures, butterfly pictures and portraits. Exhibited in London: butterfly pictures (1898), Royal Academy (1902-4), Mendoza Gallery (1906); and at Bedford Society of Artists (1899).

An Old Herbaceous Garden, Castle Close, Bedford (c. 1901)

STRATFOLD, R.C.

Fl. 1820s

Lithographer. Contributed to Revd J. D. Parry's *Select Illustrations. Historical and Topographical, of Bedfordshire* (1827).

The Grammar School, Bedford (dated1827)

TIMAEUS, F

Fl. 1840s-50s

Publisher of prints, Bedford. The Timaeus family were of Moravian extraction, and were booksellers and printers at 90 High Street, Bedford, throughout the nineteenth and the first half of the twentieth centuries. Published Henry Burn's *Bedford from the North* (c.1850-5).

BIBLIOGRAPHY

Baker, A.E., and Wilde, N.C., *Bedford in Times Past* (1980) Countryside Publications, Chorley, Lancs

Baker, David, *et al.*, 'Excavations in Bedford 1967-1977' (1979), *Bedfordshire Archaeological Journal*, Vol. 13, Bedfordshire Archaeological Council

Baker, David and Evelyn, *The Beginnings of Bedford* (1985), Bedfordshire County Planning Department

Bailey, Martin, 'Curious past of Mappa Mundi drops into place', 5 November 1989, *Observer*

Bell, Patricia, 'Surveying the County', *Bedfordshire Magazine* , Vol. 20 (1985), pp.3-9 (Thomas Jobson Jackson)

Bell, Patricia, *Belief in Bedfordshire* (1986) Belfry Press, Bedford

Bénézit, E., *Dictionnaire des Peintres, Sculpteurs, Dessinateurs et Graveurs* (1966), Librairie Grund, France

Blyth, Thomas Allen, Ph.D. (comp.), *The History of Bedford* (n.d., c.1873), Longmans, Green, Reader and Dyer, London

Bryan's Dictionary of Painters and Engravers (new edn 1903-4), G. Bell and Sons Ltd, London

Carter, Christopher ('Touchstone'), *A Picture Book of Bedford* (1951), The Mayor's Parlour, Bedford

Cashman, Bernard, *Private Charity and the Public Purse: The Development of Bedford General Hospital 1794-1988* (1988), North Bedfordshire Health Authority

Cashman, Bernard, *A Proper House, Bedford Lunatic Asylum: 1812-1860* (1992), North Bedfordshire Health Authority

Cirket, Alan F., 'The Fraser Brothers — Artists of Bedford', *Bedfordshire Magazine*, Vol. 16 (1978), pp. 273-6

Cirket, Alan F., *Souvenir Guide to the John Bunyan Museum, Library and Bunyan Meeting Free Church* (1992), Fidelity Colour, Essex

Concise Dictionary of National Biography (1939), Oxford University Press, Oxford

Conisbee, L. R., *A Bedfordshire Bibliography* (1962), Bedfordshire Historical Record Society (and supplements)

Crawley, Alan, and Freeman, Ian, 'Bedford's Oldest Streets', *Bedfordshire Archaeology*, Vol 18 (1988) and 19 (1992), Bedfordshire Archaeological Council

Farrar, The Revd C. F., *Old Bedford* (1926), F. R. Hockliffe, Bedford; Simpkin, Marshall and Co. Ltd, London

Godber, Joyce *The Harpur Trust 1552-1973* (1973), The Harpur Trust, Bedford

Godber, Joyce, *The Story of Bedford* (1978), White Crescent Press Ltd, Luton

Graves, Algernon, *A Dictionary of Artists 1760-1893* (1901), Henry Graves and Co. Ltd, London

Graves, Algernon, *The Royal Academy of Arts Exhibitors: Dictionary of Contributors, 1769-1904* (1905), Henry Graves and Co. Ltd, London (repr. 1970, S. R. Publishers, Wakefield, and Kingsmead Reprints, Bath)

Greenshields, Margaret, 'A Bedfordshire Topographer', *Bedfordshire Magazine,* Vol. 5 (1956), pp. 135-9 (Thomas Fisher)

Greenshields, Margaret, 'A Bedford Schoolmaster Artist', *Bedfordshire Magazine,* Vol. 7 (1960-1), pp. 247-50 (Bradford Rudge)

Grubert, Halina, *Cecil Higgins 1856-1941 Collector Extraordinary* (1983), Cecil Higgins Art Gallery, Bedford

Hamson, J., *Bedford Town and Townsmen* (1896), *Bedfordshire Times* office, Mill Street, Bedford

Hand, Mary, 'Some Bedfordshire Bridges', *Bedfordshire Magazine,* Vol. 12 (1970), pp. 267-8

Houfe, Simon, *The Dictionary of British Book Illustrators and Caricaturists 1800-1914* (1978), Baron Publishing, Woodbridge, Suffolk

Houfe, Simon, 'The Bedfordshire Prodigy: George Arnald ARA', *Bedfordshire Magazine,* Vol. 22 (1990), pp. 135-41

Kuhlicke, F. W., *A History of the Hospital and Parish Church of St John the Baptist, Bedford* (1961), booklet, including 'An Account of John Bunyan and St John's' by H. G. Tibbutt

Kuhlicke, F. W., 'The Bedford Mint', *Bedfordshire Magazine,* Vol. 13 (1972), pp. 167-70

Lester, Anthony J., *The Stannards of Bedfordshire* (1984), Eastbourne Fine Art Publications, Eastbourne

Lysons, The Revds David and Samuel, *Magna Britannia Vol. I* (1806), London (repr. 1978, E. P. Publishing Ltd, Wakefield)

Mackenzie, Ian, *British Prints* (1987) Antique Collectors' Club, Woodbridge, Suffolk

Mander, R. P., 'Early Theatres of Bedford', *Bedfordshire Magazine,* Vol. 3 (1951-2), pp. 92-5 (Old George Inn)

Matthiason, J. H., *Bedford and Its Environs* (1831), W. White, Bedford

Meynell, Laurence, *Bedfordshire* (1950), Robert Hale Ltd, London

Morris, Christopher (ed.), *The Journeys of Celia Fiennes* (1947), Cresset Press, London (repr. 1984 as *The Illustrated Journeys of Celia Fiennes c. 1682-c. 1712,* Macdonald, London)

Nicholls, Yvonne, 'Bradford Rudge, Artist', *Bedfordshire Magazine,* Vol. 16 (1977), pp. 101-6

Nicholson, John, *An illustrated Guide to Bunyan's Bedford* (1989), B.M.Bozo, London

Pevsner, Nikolaus, *The Buildings of England: Bedfordshire and the County of Huntingdon and Peterborough* (1968), Penguin, Harmondsworth

Redgrave, Samuel, *A Dictionary of Artists of the English School* (1878), George Bell and Sons, London

Roberts, Margery, 'Some Bedfordshire Bridges', *Bedfordshire Magazine*, Vol. 4 (1955), pp. 320-4

St John House Information Leaflet (n.d., 1980s)

Stephanopoulos, Photios, 'The Architecture of George Dance the Younger' (1972), unpublished B. Arch.(Hons.) dissertation, University of Liverpool

Stockdale, Eric, *A Study of Bedford Prison 1660-1877* (1977), Phillimore and Co., Chichester

Tibbutt, H.G., *Bunyan Meeting 1650-1950* (1950), published by the Trustees of the Bunyan Meeting, Bedford

Underwood, Andrew, *Bedford Modern School of the Black and Red* (1981), published by the school

The Victoria History of the Counties of England: A History of the County of Bedford (1904), Vols I, II and III, Archibald Constable and Co. Ltd, Westminster

Welch, Edwin (ed.), *The Bedford Moravian Church in the Eighteenth Century: A Selection of Documents* (1989), Bedfordshire Historical Record Society (Vol. 68), Bedford

White, William Hale, *The Autobiography of Mark Rutherford* (1988, first pub. 1881), Libris Ltd, London

Wildman, Richard, *Bygone Bedford* (1974), White Crescent Press Ltd, Luton

Wildman, Richard, *Bedford Past and Present* (1975), Paul Hooley and Associates, Bedford

Wildman, Richard, *Bedford: A Pictorial History* (1991), Phillimore and Co., Chichester

Wood, Christopher, *Dictionary of Victorian Painters* (1978), Antique Collectors' Club, Woodbridge, Suffolk

Additional materials from Bedfordshire County Record Office

Information leaflets: 'Pumps and Ploughs'; 'In the Shadow of the Wings'; 'Such as are Distressed and Afflicted in Minde'

Reference materials: BMB 14/A27, CRT 130 Bedford 79, CRT 130 Bedford 143, CRT 130 Bedford 157, CRT 180/99, CRT 180/144, CRT 180/195, CRT 180/324

Material from Bedford Central Library Local Studies Reference Section

Correspondence of William Hale White

Material from Cecil Higgins Art Gallery, Bedford

Thomas Fisher Scrapbook, Vol. A-CHI

INDEX

References are to plate and article numbers.

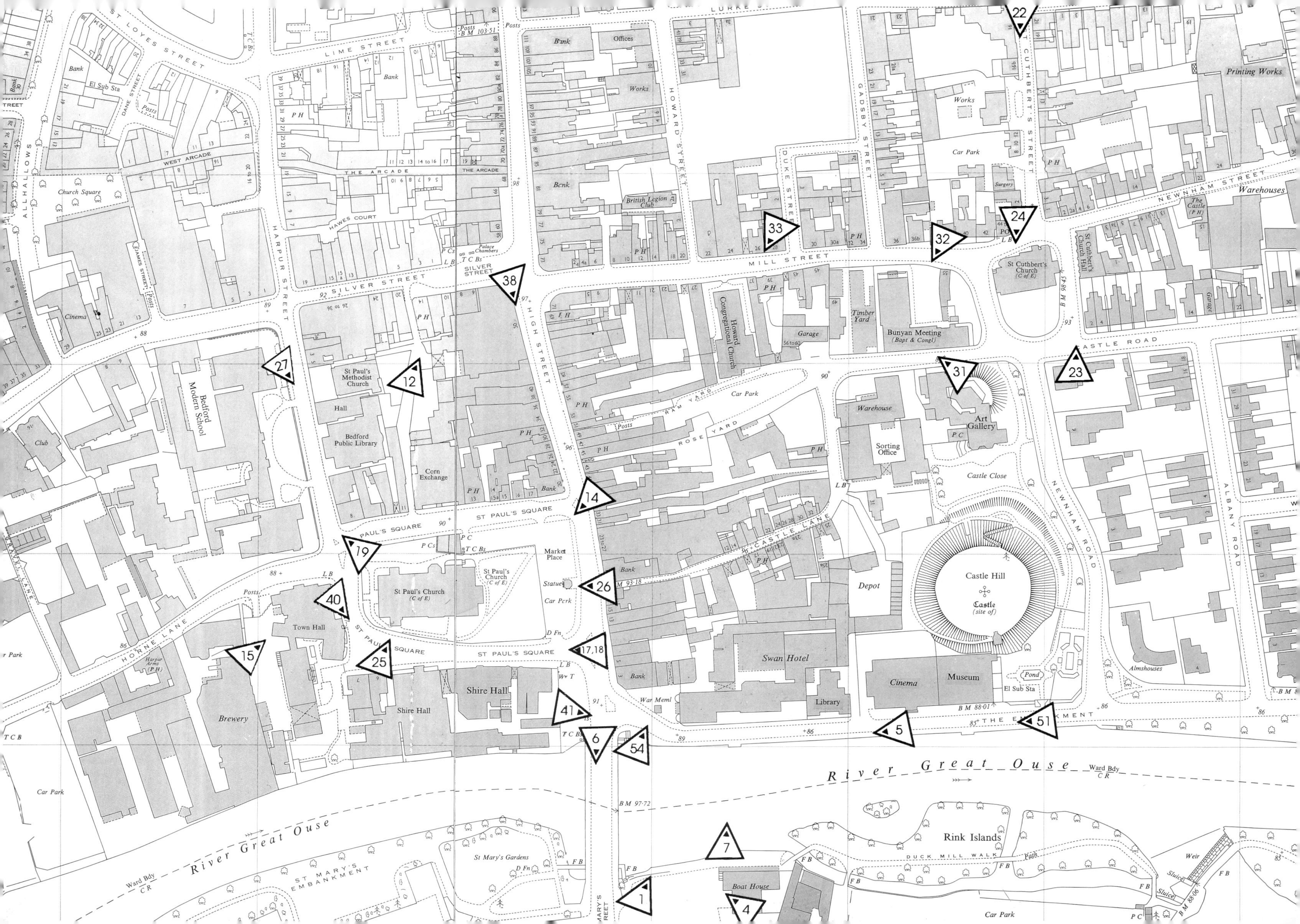

ST LOYES STREET
LIME STREET
ALLHALLOWS
Church Square
DANE STREET
El Sub Sta
Bank
WEST ARCADE
THE ARCADE
HAWES COURT
HARPUR STREET
JAMES STREET
SILVER STREET
Palace Chambers
Cinema
Bedford Modern School
Club
St Paul's Methodist Church
Hall
Bedford Public Library
Corn Exchange
ST PAUL'S SQUARE
St Paul's Church (C of E)
Market Place
Statue
Car Park
Town Hall
HORNE LANE
Harpur Arms (PH)
Brewery
Shire Hall
War Meml
HIGH STREET
Bank
Offices
Works
British Legion Club
HOWARD STREET
DUKE STREET
GADSBY STREET
MILL STREET
Howard Congregational Church
Timber Yard
Garage
Bunyan Meeting (Bapt & Congl)
RAM YARD
ROSE YARD
CASTLE LANE
Swan Hotel
Library
Depot
Cinema
Museum
Warehouse
Sorting Office
Art Gallery
Castle Close
Castle Hill
Castle (site of)
CASTLE ROAD
ST CUTHBERTS STREET
Car Park
Surgery
St Cuthbert's Church (C of E)
St Cuthbert's Church Hall
NEWNHAM STREET
The Castle (PH)
Warehouses
Printing Works
NEWNHAM ROAD
ALBANY ROAD
Almshouses
Pond
THE EMBANKMENT
River Great Ouse
Ward Bdy C R
Rink Islands
DUCK MILL WALK
Boat House
Weir
Sluice
St Mary's Gardens
ST MARY'S EMBANKMENT
ST MARY'S STREET
Car Park
22
24
32
33
38
27
12
31
23
14
19
26
40
15
25
17,18
41
6
54
5
51
7
1
4